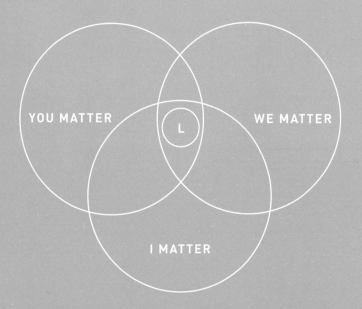

YOU MATTER

L

WE MATTER

I MATTER

PRAISE FOR YOU MATTER.

"When you first see the title *You Matter.*, you might think the book is all about you. Not so! While it *starts* with you, Matt's real goal is to help his readers create a life of purpose, meaning, and service. . . . Read *You Matter.* and absorb the important thinking of Matt Emerzian.

— **Ken Blanchard, coauthor of *The New One Minute Manager* and *Servant Leadership in Action***

"If we can all agree that our beliefs drive our behaviors, just imagine how wonderful the world would be if we all believed that we mattered, and that everyone else mattered just as much. Thanks for challenging us to think differently Matt." — **Lenny Comma CEO, Jack in the Box**

"Matt's messages are relatable to people as well as the companies in which they work. We need to make sure our people know they are valued, have purpose, and matter to our companies. And this book inspires just that. Employees who are cared for/about by their employers are able to bring their whole outstanding self to work. In addition to his written word, Zoom has had the privilege of experiencing Matt as a keynote speaker, which left many inspired souls as well as not a dry eye in the room." — **Lynne Oldham, chief people officer, Zoom Video Communications**

"*You Matter.* is a story for and about all of us. Matt's willingness to share his own journey of brokenness reminds us that this life isn't easy, and finding purpose is necessary. Matt provides us a pathway to that purpose by exemplifying a life of meaningful connection and joy." — **Scott Harrison, *New York Times* bestselling author of *Thirst***

"I've watched Matt's transformative journey with my own eyes and seen him grow into a leader who transforms other leaders. How we treat people along our own life's path *matters*, and Matt's personal example is one I plan to follow. You should too. We'll all thank you." — **Thomas Greanias, *New York Times* bestselling author of *Raising Atlantis***

"In today's tech-obsessed world, it's easy to fall into the compare-and-despair trap. We focus a great deal on "succeeding" without stopping to think about what that really means. *You Matter.* shifts the framework and helps us think about what it means to thrive."

—**Jessica Abo**, **author of** *Unfiltered:*
How to Be as Happy as You Look on Social Media

"Read this book. Matthew will inspire and transform you through his own powerful story. Whether through the pages of this book or Matthew sharing on a stage, he's a Catalyst and change agent! Bring him in to speak to your team, staff, network, or conference. You can be confident that leaders will leave more inspired and ultimately transformed to make a difference and lead well in any environment. Companies, nonprofits, schools, churches, and teams need this message!"

—**Brad Lomenick, founder of BLINC and**
author of *H3 Leadership* **and** *The Catalyst Leader*

"If you struggle bringing meaning into your life and you aren't fully living a life with your specific purpose in mind—this book is for you. Allow Matthew, in his lovely book, to guide you to a personal discovery that leads you to your greater self. You Matter. This book Matters."

—**Chris Chalk, actor, writer, and filmmaker of**
When They See Us, Gotham, Farewell, **and** *Perry Mason*

"Matthew's book is pure joy. It forces you to just stop, take a deep breath and be/live in the moment, a moment that is precious. Life is fast. Fleeting. Challenging. We are all doing the best we can. . . . Do yourself a favor and take some time and read this glorious book. It matters, and most of all, YOU MATTER!!"   —**Lawrence Zarian, author of**
Lawrence Zarian's 10 Commandments
for a Perfect Wardrobe **and lifestyle expert**
on *Live with Kelly and Ryan* **and** *Home and Family*

"*You Matter.* is the breath of fresh air we so desperately need. We live in a culture of exhausting ambition, but Matthew shows us that we don't have to earn the right to be valuable or worthwhile—we already are."

—**Alexis Jones, speaker, activist, and author of** *I Am That Girl*

"Want to motivate your co-workers to find true purpose in what they do each day? Look no further. His passion and vision will unleash your potential, helping you and your team change the world around you for the better!"   —**Cammie Cannella, vice president**
global education and customer experience, **Kiehl's**

YOU MATTER.

ALSO BY MATTHEW EMERZIAN

Every Monday Matters

LEARNING TO LOVE
WHO YOU REALLY ARE

Matthew Emerzian

ST. MARTIN'S
ESSENTIALS
NEW YORK

TO MY WIFE, PATTY,
I LOVE YOU.

First published in the United States by St. Martin's Essentials, an imprint of St. Martin's Publishing Group

YOU MATTER. Copyright © 2020 by Matthew Emerzian. Foreword copyright © 2020 by Ken Blanchard. All rights reserved. Printed in the United States of America. For information, address St. Martin's Publishing Group, 120 Broadway, New York, NY 10271.

www.stmartins.com

The Library of Congress Cataloging-in-Publication Data is available upon request.

ISBN 978-1-250-20999-3 (hardcover)
ISBN 978-1-250-61937-2 (ebook)

Our books may be purchased in bulk for promotional, educational, or business use. Please contact your local bookseller or the Macmillan Corporate and Premium Sales Department at 1-800-221-7945, extension 5442, or by email at MacmillanSpecialMarkets@macmillan.com.

First Edition: February 2020

10 9 8 7 6 5 4 3 2 1

CONTENTS

FOREWORD

When Matt Emerzian asked me to write a foreword for *You Matter.*, I was thrilled because I'm a raving fan of Matt. He's a very special human being who cares about people and wants to make a difference in their lives. Matt rose up from being down and out, even contemplating suicide, to realize that he mattered and could make a difference in the world.

When you first see the title *You Matter.*, you might think the book is all about you. Not so! While it *starts* with you, Matt's real goal is to help his readers create a life of purpose, meaning, and service. That last word is key: *service*. When you finally understand that *you matter*, as Matt emphasizes, your focus is no longer on yourself but on making a difference in the lives of others. That outlook is consistent with what I have found in working with and observing business leaders for more than forty years. Let me explain.

I've met a lot of managers who are control freaks that think all the brains are in their office. They expect people to suck up to the hierarchy and follow orders. Why are they like that? Because their need to control is a way of overcompensating for not-okay feelings about themselves. They are scared little kids inside who don't have a clue that they really *matter*.

On the other hand, great managers generate great loyalty

and produce great results. They are comfortable serving others rather than being served. Why are they like that? Because as servant leaders, they realize that being an effective leader is not about them, it's about the people they serve. They feel good about themselves—in Matt's terms, they understand that they *matter*.

Matt has made a career out of helping people understand that they matter. That's why I invited him to speak at both our company-wide and customer-wide conferences. And boy, did he make a difference!

Read *You Matter.* and absorb the important thinking of Matt Emerzian. Once you understand that *you* matter, you can create a culture in your home, your organization, and your community where everyone understands that *they* matter, too.

Thanks, Matt, for helping me realize that I matter and we matter. And I certainly know that *you* matter!

—Ken Blanchard, coauthor of
The New One Minute Manager
and *Servant Leadership in Action*

PREFACE

It's not about you.

These are the first four words from one of the best-selling books of all time.

They remind us that in order to discover what most stirs our heart, ignites our passion, and elevates our lives, we must begin with the surprising truth that it's just not about us. It turns out that to gain the best of our lives we must let go of the reigns believing that it's all about what we want for our lives.

Matt Emerzian understands this. He teaches this. Because he lived this.

Upon graduating from UCLA with his MBA, Matt got his dream job. Hired as a senior vice president at a major music marketing company, he worked directly with and on projects for some of the biggest celebrities in the world. Matt was successful, hung out with the biggest names in music and showbiz, and was invited to the most exclusive parties.

He was on top of the world and had it all. Yet felt as if he was at the bottom of it where very little of it actually even mattered.

Seeking greater meaning, Matt discovered that all of the success, the parties, and the fame did nothing to fill a gaping hole in his life. He remained unhappy, unfulfilled, and became clinically depressed.

After numerous counseling sessions, he was given a simple book to read to improve his spirits. The first four words surprised him: *It's not about you.*

This was a viewpoint an athletic, handsome, successful but discontented Hollywood guy never even considered. Up until that point, candidly, it was all about him.

Matt pivoted and began volunteering. He sought opportunities to serve pursuing occasions to find the value within others and encourage them to see it within themselves. He inspired others to recognize that they had value, that they were deserving of love and respect, that they mattered.

Gradually, something dramatic happened within how he viewed his life. Matt began to appreciate his own unique gifts, he embraced his own self-worth and he finally recognized the profound blessings within his life. He came to know that he truly mattered.

In the book, *You Matter.: Learning to Love Who You Really Are,* Matt Emerzian shares a beautiful and simple construct you can leverage to improve your relationships, your professional journey, and your personal life. He shares the mighty disconnect between striving for temporary success and obtaining true significance. He unpacks the great difference between pursuing what is fleetingly valuable rather than obtaining and celebrating the priceless.

Have you ever wondered, "Do I truly matter?" Have you ever sought to make a difference, impact other lives? Have you ever desired to unlock greater meaning, purpose, and passion in your life?

Reading this book will remind you that you are not alone asking these questions and will inspire you to undeniably answer them with certainty that *You Matter*. Through that belief you'll learn to love who you really are and embrace the calling of your life.

And with love as fuel you'll have not only the courage to act on that calling, but the assurance that those lucky enough to encounter you may know for certain that they matter, too.

This book is an awesome reminder that You Matter.

Now it's time to act like it.

> —John O'Leary, #1 national
> bestselling author of *On Fire*
> and host of the Live Inspired
> podcast

Introduction

FALLING FORWARD

Do you feel things deeply?

If you are like me, you are a very sensitive person. Sometimes I think it's a curse. For many very dark years, it felt like a bad one. But today I see it differently. I see it as a badge of honor, because I now know what it feels like to be human, and it allows me to see and feel things in other people that I never felt before. No, I am not an energy healer or a psychic or anything like that. But I am someone who has felt deep brokenness, anxiety, and depression. I am someone who has run the gamut of "Life is good" to "Life is horrible and hard" to "Wow, this is what life is about? This is better than I could have imagined."

For the past ten years, I have traveled the country sharing my story on stages in front of fifty to five thousand people. I have spoken to students, educators, employees, executives, criminals, veterans, victims of domestic violence, churchgoers, volunteers, influencers, and TED goers, and my message didn't change. I believe that we humans are all the same: we want to feel loved, know that our life has purpose and meaning, be seen and heard, have gifts to offer the world, be worthy and enough, have our words and actions be meaningful, and know we are special. The challenge is that many of us don't feel this way. I know, because I was one of them. But I also know that all of us can . . . and we will.

In this book, I'll tell you some of my story in the introduction, so you know where I'm coming from. And then in parts 1, 2, and 3 we will together dive into the ideas and steps it takes to know your worth and the value of your life. I'll share some stories from my life and the lives of those I've met over the years.

I also suggest you get a journal to keep handy while you read this book. In the three parts after the introduction, I offer positive action steps to take, some journal prompts to help you reflect on the message of that chapter, as well as some conversation starters so you and a friend or group don't just read these words but also discuss them. Use these action items, journal prompts, and conversation starters as ways to figure out how to apply the ideas in this book to your life. Reading the book is a good thing; applying the messages to your own life is a transformative thing. Much like telling you that You Matter is much different from you experiencing it firsthand.

I wrote this book with big hopes for you. I hope that this book introduces you to deeper understandings about yourself and your choices. That it empowers you to "go there," while shining a light on tough topics, both personally and socially. That the stories I share will make you smile, laugh, cry, dream, and everything in between, just as they did for me when I lived them. And, most important, that when you finish reading the last word, not only are you inspired and encouraged, but transformed. Because you matter. Once you own this, your life will change forever. And when enough of us own this, we will change the world.

That is my hope for you and the world.

You matter.

LIFE FOREVER CHANGED

My rock bottom happened on a Monday morning.

As I tied my Chuck Taylors while getting ready for work on just another Monday morning, I could tell something was different. I felt it the moment I opened my eyes, but I didn't know what it was. It was a sensation I had never experienced before, which only heightened my discomfort and exacerbated the symptoms. Was I getting sick? Maybe the flu? No, this was different. Heavier. Dread-filled.

As I slowly sat up from the pine trunk at the end of my bed, almost afraid to look up and check in with my surroundings and myself, it hit. My vision tunneled, my heart started racing, sweat drops beaded up on my arms and forehead, and my breathing immediately shortened. I was in trauma.

Could this be a heart attack? Was I dying? Was this going to be my day? Home alone and scared, I ran out the front door to see if any of my neighbors were home. I needed help. My first thought of course was to call 911, but then I was concerned they would show up at my house to find a dead thirty-one-year-old lying cold on the wood floors of his home. I thought it might be faster to just drive to my doctor's office. I jumped in my car and, as I was headed there, I began talking myself off the ledge. *Matt, just calm down. You are healthy. You would have died already if it were something major.* I convinced myself that I was going to be okay. Feeling better for the moment, instead of driving to my doctor, I decided to head toward my parents' house.

Clearly my thinking was mixed up. For starters, they lived five hours away without traffic. But it was 8:00 A.M. in Southern California, so with morning rush hour the trip was going to be more like a seven-hour drive. As soon as I hit bumper-to-bumper traffic on the freeway, I burst into tears. I completely fell apart. The panic was back stronger than ever.

I tried calling my parents but was unable to get a single word out. I was stuck—unable to see through the tears and stopped dead in the middle lane of a typical SoCal five-lane-wide freeway.

At this point my symptoms were unbearable. I somehow forced my way off the freeway, driving on the median until I reached the exit, and quickly headed for my doctor's office again.

Reaching my doctor's office was like discovering an oasis in the desert. I was no longer alone. Still scared, but not alone. The caregivers started in with the blood pressure cuff, then a needle in my elbow joint, and multiple vials of blood drawn, a stethoscope down my shirt, and a cup for me to pee in. It was hard for me to concentrate or even sit still enough to allow them to do their job. Their comments echoed in my ears: "Just try to relax" and "Everything is going to be okay" and "Breathe, Matt."

Finally, my doctor walked into the small exam room that felt no larger than a broom closet. Warm, caring, and witty, he had a certain way of always calming me, so seeing his face and hearing his voice were instant comfort for me.

"Matt, you are not having a heart attack; your heart is totally healthy," he said.

Relieved but confused, I realized his comments raised new unanswered questions.

"Then what is wrong with me?" I asked. "I've never felt anything like this before."

My doctor started asking me about my life. He asked how work was going, how my personal life was, and about my habits. We talked about the importance of balance and rest and healthy life choices. Everything we spoke about had less to do with my physical heart and more to do with my emotional and mental heart—that vulnerable place deep inside us that we so often keep hidden.

His advice for me was to go home and rest. Once I felt better, in the days ahead, he wanted me to take time to ask the tough questions about life and significance and purpose and meaning. When I asked why a medical doctor was asking me to think through these questions, he delivered the diagnosis.

"You're clinically depressed and suffering from chronic

anxiety disorder," he said. "Whatever you're doing needs to change."

Little did I know, from that Monday morning on, my life would be forever changed.

OUR DEEPEST NEED, MY GREATEST MISSION

I believe we are brought into this world with the same set of hopes—to be good and to feel good. We are human beings, considered by us the masters of the universe . . . and any other universe, for that matter. We want to be happy. We want to be healthy. We avoid hurt at all costs. We have all seen the workout posters: NO PAIN, NO GAIN. We would rather that they say, "NO PAIN, NO PAIN." Isn't that easier? Avoiding pain or danger is in our DNA. It's called, "fight or flight." And given the choice, we would never encounter circumstances that caused them to surface.

Our greatest fear is dying. If we had it our way, we would never die—and we are trying to discover how to make that a reality at a feverish pace. The antiaging industry is currently over $150 billion a year and is projected to surpass the $300 billion mark in the next few years. We have Botox, antiwrinkle products, antistretch products, antipigmentation therapy, liposuction, chemical peels, oxygen chambers, vitamin shots, hair restoration treatments, microdermabrasion, laser aesthetics, anticellulite treatments, and antiaging radio-frequency devices, just to

name a few products and procedures. Anything and everything for us to stay young—even if it means injecting
ourselves with poisons to do so. But this only speaks to the
physical side of the equation, and, frankly, I'm yet to meet
someone who has beat Father Time.

What about the mental and emotional parts of life? I
believe we also want to be happy. We want our lives to be
filled with joy. In the beginning of life, we were pretty good
at this. Life was good: we ate, pooped, and slept. We were
innocent and life was one big discovery, filled with awe and
wonder.

At a certain age, the innocence drifted away and our
awareness shifted. Life was still good, but it got a little
more complicated. We started to experience new feelings,
thoughts, and changes. We became aware, both individually and socially. Then middle and high school—those six
years, from seventh to twelfth grades, have growing pains
written all over them. Our bodies changed. We discovered
certain organs and how they make us feel. We had to perform well to get to the next level, be it in sports, school,
or other social constructs. We enjoyed our first slow dance
and first kiss. We also survived our first heartbreak.

If this wasn't already enough, we had "friendly" com-
petitions for homecoming, prom, yearbook nominations,
National Honor Society, and student government, and our
sense of value and worth were put on trial again. The com-
paring and competing began, thereby developing insecurities all along the way, and we began building our own little
private, safe bubbles to hide our wounds.

After high school, we continued to follow the rules. We went to college, got a job, hoped to get married and build the perfect life. All along, making our parents proud and judging those who didn't do everything "right."

But what happened? *Because I certainly don't feel fulfilled. I have endured an overwhelming amount of performance pressure. I am in debt. And I am one of the "lucky" ones who actually secured a job, unlike a lot of my friends who followed the rules as well. Why didn't anyone actually tell us the whole story? How is it that there are high school dropouts who are now multimillionaires? How is it that there are Instagram and YouTube stars making millions of dollars by simply expressing themselves? Why didn't someone tell me that life would be filled with letdowns, broken hearts, failures, broken promises, and hurt? Or why was their only answer to saddle up, grow some skin, and know that past generations had it even worse—snow, barefoot, uphill both ways. Life is hard and often sucks.* The walls of our bubbles grow thicker, and we start to go inward because we think it's safer there.

As we struggle individually and privately, we look outward, at arm's length, for the answers, but we just encounter more questions: *Where did the good guys like Mr. Rogers go? How could Bill Cosby, America's dad, have done that? How is it possible that Robin Williams committed suicide? Are cops racists? Do politicians even care about me, or just about getting my vote? Did we really elect a president that brags about grabbing pussy? Am I safe to go to flea markets, school, concerts, or to fly on an airplane anymore? Is our environment in peril? Is bigger, stronger, faster really better? Why does everyone ask me what I do instead of who I am? Does success equal money, power, influence, and popularity? Where do I rank? Why isn't being a teacher celebrated? Or what about a social worker? Is fame and wealth only for professional athletes, celebrities, and politicians? Is it "millionaire or bust" in America? Is that the dream? What happened to joy, purpose, fulfillment, peace, relationships, or happiness? I just want to feel good—and I don't. I'm tired and just want to disappear.* As the walls of our bubbles grow even thicker, we find ourselves alone, confused, and completely disconnected from ourselves and the world around us. And if all of this isn't enough to break us, our self-imposed isolation certainly will.

Now, I am fully aware that not everyone asks these questions, and this may all sound a little overdramatic to some. I also know that we all have different journeys that start in different places. But I wholeheartedly believe that there is not a single soul alive who has not stumbled upon some of these realities during his or her life's journey and that each one of us wants to be and feel healthy and happy.

This is why my mission in life is to help people know how much and why they matter. What could be more important?

OUR WORLD NEEDS IT

Just flip on the news at night and you'll get plenty of stories that show our humanity struggling. What is most newsworthy to me is that nearly every tragic story we see or read about is the result of a person, another human being, acting out. A person. A human. And if we roll back the tape and get some context, I am certain we will find one of two types of people. It will be someone who doesn't think he or she matters and feels the same about everyone else in the world. That type of person is likely apathetic, depressed, uncaring, and has given up hope. *Let someone else deal with it. What do I care? Not my problem.* Or it will be someone who actually believes he or she matters, but for all the wrong reasons. They are likely egotistical, narcissistic, lacking regard for others, and overflowing in self-entitlement. *Do you know who I am? I am wealthy. I am powerful. I play by my own rules. I'm untouchable.* Very different types of people that share the same struggle—not knowing how much and why they really matter. And the results are what we see today.

I understand this because at different times in my life, I was both of these people. I've been narcissistic and I've been depressed. I've been uncaring and I've only cared about success. I don't think this makes me bad. I just think it makes me human. But I've changed, which leads me to believe that we can all change.

WE NEED IT

We were born for something different from this. *You* were born for something different from this. Something bigger. You want to be good, do good, feel good. It's in all of us. But maybe you have lost your way a little bit. Maybe you are struggling to find purpose and meaning. Maybe you don't have as many good days as you would like. Maybe you are going through a tough transition in life. Maybe you've never embraced how amazing you are. Maybe you had a tough childhood. Maybe you are going into the second half of your life and are looking for more. Or maybe you hit rock bottom, like I did.

The fact is that you would not be reading this book if you weren't looking for something that isn't there already. If there wasn't some sort of hole in your heart or ache in your soul, coupled with a hope and a belief that there might be answers out there somewhere. Well, first let me congratulate you for having the courage to go looking for those answers. I commend you for that, for sure. That is a big and bold step. Second, let me tell you that my hope is that this book brings you some or all of the answers you are looking for. I want nothing more than for you to embrace how much and why you matter—to love and be loved, to feel like you belong, and to have hope, to have purpose, to like the person you see in the mirror both inside and outside, to embrace how powerful you are, to leave a legacy, and to know that your life has meaning . . . and that the world is all the better because of you.

CHOICES

Being human is tricky. Part of this is ultimately because we never chose this life. It's not as if one day we decided to be born and, next thing we knew, we were taking our first breath. Nope. That's not how it worked. But just because we didn't choose to be born doesn't mean we don't get to choose how to live.

We have all heard the saying "Life is full of choices." I can hear the game show *Let's Make a Deal* ringing in my ears now: "What's behind door number three, Johnny?" The average adult makes more than thirty-five thousand choices per day. Over a year, that's more than twelve million choices—over a lifetime, just under one billion. Of course, many of these decisions don't have a profound impact on the direction of our life. I'm not sure if whether I wore black or blue socks one day will determine much about my future. However, many of our choices do.

In the summer of 1997, I had to make one of those big choices. I had just graduated from the Anderson School of Management at UCLA with my MBA, and I had a career decision to make. I had interviewed with several companies and had some options on the table, but my heart wasn't really into any of them. Sure, having those three letters after my name could afford me an attractive salary, but I wasn't feeling the passion for the work. The truth is that I never really felt like I belonged in business school, and every day I questioned why I was there. But, at this point in my life, I was used to struggling to find my path: it seemed to be the story of much of my life. Ultimately, however, I needed to make a choice with the hope that, this time, I would get it right . . . but would I?

On a beautiful evening in early fall, my friends, Andrew

and Dave, invited me over to their apartment to watch Monday Night Football with a group of buddies. Little did I know, they had a plan. After priming me with pizza, beer, and something else that makes you feel a little funny after smoking it, they popped the question—"Matt, we want you to manage our band. You in?" In that moment, the seas parted, the stars aligned, and Matt officially found his purpose in life. We signed an official contract on a Domino's Pizza napkin and the rest is history. My job was to make Virgil the next U2. No biggie.

We worked hard and the guys killed it in the studio and on stage, which landed us a multimillion-dollar record deal. However, after a few months of receiving checks from the label, the money stopped coming in. I couldn't get anyone from the label on the phone. Panic settled into our camp. The guys needed this monthly check to pay their bills, to pay for band expenses, to eat. Clearly something was not up to par, and the wind was sucked out of our sails. After weeks of trying, I finally figured out that the label lost its funding and was shutting down. No more millions of dollars. No more multiple albums. Dreams squashed. Grown men upside down. Dirty businesspeople ruining lives. I was at a complete loss over what to do.

At this time, it was recommended that I meet Robert Kardashian. I only knew of his face and name from the O. J. Simpson trial. I knew him as a lawyer on the "Dream Team." What I didn't know is that Robert started and ran a successful music marketing company and had actually stopped practicing law in the seventies. The reason he was a part of the O. J. case was because he and O. J. were close friends from college at USC.

The plan was to meet Robert Kardashian because he had contracts with every major and indie record label at the time. If I could befriend him, maybe he could help me connect Virgil, and other artists, to record labels. I guess in some ways, I saw it as a farm system: I would bring the talent, he would bring the deals. Together, we could launch careers and make dreams come true.

I remember my first meeting with Robert like it was yesterday. I remember his big smile, his welcoming eyes, that silver streak in his hair, and his humor. I remember him taking me back to his office, which had walls covered in gold- and platinum-record awards and a life-size cardboard cutout of The Beatles.

Robert was kind and generous with me from the first moment we met. When we sat in his office he asked, "So who are you and how can I help you?" I shared with him that I was a band manager with a plan to build mega-acts, and I thought he and I could work together to make it happen. I also played him a few demos of different artists, but mainly with the goal of him falling in love with Virgil.

Unfortunately, Robert did not fall in love with the music, but he did fall for me and he offered me a job as vice president of his music marketing company, an offer I said yes to.

Working for Robert meant experiencing the music industry on an entirely different level. He knew everyone, and everyone knew and loved him. We had a small team, which often included the kids—Kim, Kourtney, Khloé, and even little Robert, Jr. We produced a radio show, we promoted music videos on the big screens in theaters, and we produced DVD releases and live events. I found myself working on projects for every major and indie label. More specifically, on projects for artists such as U2, Coldplay, Snow Patrol, Keane, Avril Lavigne, Black Eyed Peas, Tim McGraw, and the list goes on.

During the day, I worked in the office, which often included sightings from the kids' famous friends and the crazy energy they brought into the day. Then after work, I was either working with Virgil or attending some sort of celebrity dinner or event. These dinners and events often led to after-parties, and then after-after-parties. This lifestyle was certainly the inspiration for the hit HBO show *Entourage,* and I found myself right in the middle of it— drinking, smoking, objectifying women, staying up late, and trying to be cool in the City of Angels.

It was a slippery slope, and I was sliding with the best of them. Somehow the business kind of grooms you this way. So much ego and narcissism. So much brokenness and so many dirty deals. Yet so much glamour and so many bright lights. The red carpet and the Hollywood Hills were the places for VIPs, so that's where I started hanging out.

To further feed the beast, I would go home to Modesto, California, where I grew up, and everyone wanted to hear my stories. After all, things like this never happen in the small agricultural town of Modesto. We swam in canals and partied in orchards for fun.

Being close to this level of celebrity made me feel more important than I was. It fed my notion of "success," which is really most Americans' understanding of the word. I looked at the fame and popularity around me and thought, "This matters." I looked at my new celebrity friends and thought, "They matter." I looked at the screaming fans and thought, "That matters." And all of this made me finally think, "I matter . . . right?"

But underneath the veneer of importance, a gnawing sense of emptiness started to linger inside of me. I painfully realized I had grown lonely in my relationships, most of which were shallow and superficial. Then one sun-drenched Saturday afternoon I found myself at a pool party in the Hollywood Hills, filled with celebrities and models and millionaires—the typical fare. Sitting by the pool, I started looking around and observing the crowd. I noticed that many of the people at the party were likely in their fifties, yet they were still performing and pretending to seem and feel important. *Is this where I would be in twenty years? Was I destined to become that desperate guy one day?*

A weird feeling began to build inside me, and I got up from my poolside lounger and grabbed the keys to my car from the valet. Racing off the property, I got into my car and sped home. The sensation had subsided by the time I arrived, but the peace would not last. I was beginning to realize I had been chasing after smoke and wind. I was starting to question everything, including my own worth. And unbeknownst to me, I was about to have a complete mental breakdown.

A few weeks later, I was set up on a blind date with a woman that several mutual friends thought would be "the one" for me. I am embarrassed to say that I don't remember her name, and I don't even remember the name of the restaurant. I remember she was sweet, kind, and pretty, but I also remember immediately thinking she was not the one. More significantly, though, I remember that the feeling came back again—the same "I need to get the hell out of here" feeling that I had just experienced at that Hollywood pool party. The sweat started dripping down my back, my legs started to feel weak, my hands became clammy, and my vision started to tunnel. I quickly tried to drink more of my cocktail to calm me down, but I couldn't fight the feeling, and I needed to leave. I felt terrible for cutting the date so short, and a bit concerned about what she would say to our mutual friends who thought we would be perfect together, but I needed to get home and get to bed. I just wanted to sleep it off.

Unfortunately, a little sleep couldn't stop what was about to happen the next morning—the Monday that changed my life forever.

MY EXPENSIVE FRIEND

A month after that Monday morning from hell, things were still not going well. In fact, it got much worse. I refused to take any medications the doctor recommended for me, thinking everything would pass and I would be back on the slippery slope of my work again. I guess when the doctor told me that "whatever I was doing needed to change," he actually meant it. The hard part is that the eye cannot see itself, so it was hard to know what I was doing and what needed changing.

At that point, my "dream" life was crashing down. I failed everything and everyone. My appetite had vanished. Sleep evaded me. The paranoia got so bad at night that I needed to shut all of the blinds in my home to deflect the feeling that the sky and the darkness were closing in on me. Driving my car became too stressful because I knew I wouldn't be able to handle a traffic jam, short of leaving my car in the middle of the road and running home. I also had this real fear of taking my car up to 80 mph and simply yanking the wheel to end my anguish. I was literally that desperate.

Thankfully, my parents made the executive decision to spend a month with me. My dad came down from Modesto first for two weeks, and then they traded duties. I remember my father driving me to my first counseling appointment. I was not happy at all. I could feel my core body temperature skyrocketing—partly from anger, partly from fear, partly from embarrassment—not the best places from which to operate. At the same time, I remember the feeling of surrender. Acknowledging that I needed help, and thank God I had my loving mom and dad there to hold my hand and lead the way.

My therapist's name is Denise. She and I spent several hours together that day. And the next day. And for many days over the weeks, months, and years to come. I got lucky, because I knew from the very first minute that she was the right therapist and coach for me. I could tell she was going to be empathetic and compassionate, but she was no pushover and was going to call me out on my "stuff." Perfect.

Denise and I made an unofficial, unspoken agreement. I would pay for her daughters' college educations and she would save my life. I think the deal worked out nicely for everyone. I called her "My Expensive Friend." In the beginning, it was all about slowing down the water that was crashing onboard. The ship was sinking quickly and we needed to plug a ton of holes. Once we leveled things out a bit through months of hard work, we systematically worked through my life, my views, my feelings, my motivations, my goals, my needs.

One day Denise told me she wanted to give my recovery a motto, and she slid a book across the table to me. She asked me to read the first sentence of the book, which is: **"It's not about you."**

You might have read this line before from Rick Warren's book *The Purpose Driven Life*. Denise then said, "Matt, until you understand what it means to live a life not about you, you are never going to feel better." Interesting. Foreign. Confusing. How is it possible that I am sitting here depressed, riddled with anxiety, having occasional suicidal thoughts, yet it's not about me? All of a sudden, one plus one didn't equal two. Besides the fact that I was the one hurting, I was also the one seeking her help. A narcissist working in the most narcissistic industry in the world. How can this possibly not be about me?

The next thing I remember is that week after week, for months, I spent my Saturday mornings doing something that wasn't about me. A new addition to my recovery tonic: I fed homeless people. I read to elderly. I picked up trash, painted over graffiti, wrote letters to veterans. For some reason, my jam became picking up litter. There was something about being out on the town Saturday mornings that was so peaceful. The city was still sleeping. I got to know the Meals on Wheels drivers, the dog walkers, the early crew at Starbucks. I didn't wear headphones or listen to music, rather I was just super present with the sights, sounds, and even smells of walking the streets and picking up other people's trash. Just me, my rubber gloves, garbage bags, baseball cap pulled low, and big sunglasses. Of course, I still had a reputation to protect.

One Saturday morning while picking up litter, I got a phone call from some friends who worked in PR. They were going up to a pool party in the Hollywood Hills. Sound familiar? They asked me to join them, and I blurted out, "No thanks, I am out picking up litter. I'm good."

I hung up the phone and thought, "Holy crap, I just outed my secret. My sickness." Only my family and one of my closest friends knew about my situation, and that just changed.

But then, in a moment of magic, lightning bolts, God, aha, it all clicked for me. The motto Denise gave for my recovery finally made sense. I realized that it was actually possible to find more meaning, purpose, and significance picking up other people's litter than it was doing everything else I did all week. That by being of service to others, I could find myself. That living a life not about me would actually lead me to me.

It was that moment when hope reentered my life. It was that moment, when I started believing that I could actually live a long, healthy life free from the pain, worry, anxiety, depression, and darkness that had taken over my life for years. I finally saw the way to live a life that mattered, and I couldn't wait to share it with the world, because I know I wasn't alone on this journey called "life."

FROM BROKENNESS TO BLESSING

A few weeks after my profound moment standing on the sidewalk of Wilshire Boulevard, trash bags in hand, rubber gloves on, and empowered by a new understanding of the meaning of life, I was walking back to my office with a coworker and noticed a piece of litter in the street gutter. In his defense, he had no idea I was a secret semiprofessional trash picker-upper every Saturday morning, so instinctively I bent down and picked up the crinkled piece of paper. At that moment, my coworker asked me why I would pick up someone else's trash. I tried to explain by sharing a bit of this breakthrough I had experienced a few weeks prior, but the conversation ended quickly with an argument and him saying, "Dude, you're weird."

Pissed off, I went up to my office and called my friend Kelly to share an idea that popped into my mind. "Kelly, it's Matt; I want to write a book," I shared excitedly. She responded with, "Matt, you don't even read books; how are you going to write one?" There was some truth to her reply, but I went on to explain that I wanted to write a book that shows us ordinary people that we matter. That every single one of us matters. And that together we can change the world.

My thought was, if it took me one second to pick up one piece of litter, what if all 300+ million people in our country picked up just one? It would still be a collective one second, but 300+ million pieces of litter would be gone. What if we each picked up five or ten? Or what if we got our schools, companies, churches, friends, or family involved? It is just a numbers game.

What if we all smiled more, planted a tree, donated blood, wrote a note of gratitude, took better care of our health? It just became a "What if" game. I wanted to call the book *Why Wouldn't You?* The actions I wanted to put in the book were so simple for people to do, why wouldn't they want to do them? Kelly and I started making a list of "Why wouldn't you?" actions, and we immediately had over 100 of them. Eventually the list got to 150.

One day my father called me to offer his opinion on the book. He said, "You know, I believe your working title is too negative and not inspiring enough. I think you should go with something more upbeat and positive, like *Every Monday Matters*." Bam. The book got a new name. Let's help people start their weeks off inspired. No more TGIF, which has always been one of the dumbest concepts to me. The fact that we even have a restaurant chain named after it boggles my mind. Living doesn't only happen from Friday evening to Sunday around 1:00 P.M. when we start dreading the next Monday on the horizon. Living starts at the beginning of the week, and we take it up a level each day.

We picked fifty-two actions from our list and wrote the book *Every Monday Matters: 52 Ways to Make a Difference,* and amazingly it was acquired by a publisher. It was a simple guide to help people engage in something bigger than them every week. Sounds a bit familiar to what Denise had me do, doesn't it? If it worked for me, it just might work for someone else, too. We were going to find out soon enough.

A month after the book came out, I received an email from a single mother named Darby, who shared a story that she was driving down the road and saw a car pulled over with a woman hanging out of the door. Darby pulled over to see if the woman was having car trouble. What she learned was that she was not having car trouble, rather she was there to commit suicide. She was just waiting to get up the courage to jump in front of an oncoming car. Instead, Darby showed up. In her email, Darby included the copy from a thank-you note the woman had sent to her for saving her life. And at the end of that, Darby wrote, "If it weren't for your book, I would have never pulled over to help."

I never dreamed of writing a book, let alone one that would literally save somebody's life. But that was the sign I needed to walk away from the music industry and try to make Every Monday Matters a household idea. To finally live a life that matters.

It started with just me, then unemployed and working from home. Thank God Subway had started their $5 Footlong program. Subway for lunch and dinner for $10. Bargain. Little by little it started to grow. I created a Myspace page and people started joining in. *Poor Myspace . . . at least it was good for EMM.* I was asked to write a newspaper column for *The Modesto Bee.* Massive readership, for sure. The column was then syndicated to papers all across the country. From music exec to "Dear Abby" . . . who would have thunk it? Then I received an email from Harpo Productions. Unbeknownst to me, Forest Whitaker, the actor, bought my book and took it to President Obama's first inauguration in DC, where Forest handed it to Oprah. *What? Oprah!* I ended up doing a year-long partnership with Harpo, which showcased a new Monday on Oprah.com and on her *Spirit* newsletter.

All of a sudden, I found myself running a small "movement" out of my home. I say the word "movement" loosely, because I believe it is overused, often inaccurately, but I certainly wasn't running a business yet, so I had to call it something. But then a few key developments turned the book into an actual company.

Teachers who purchased the book started emailing me asking for lesson plans, as they wanted their students to learn this concept of self- and social responsibility. So we partnered with a group of educators in Central California to create the EMM K–12 Education Program and began selling it. Additionally, companies for which I had keynoted started asking for more. They wanted team-building experiences, employee engagement, and corporate-culture work, so we launched the EMM Corporate Engagement Program and started working with companies nationwide. Every Monday Matters now had office space, employees, payroll, health care. Somehow, in a wild tail-wagging-the-dog fashion, EMM had become something. But just when everything seemed to have settled into place and had found a rhythm, another moment happened that changed me again. I was asked to speak to a group of convicted felons who were using *Every Monday Matters,* the book, as part of a restorative justice program.

I will never forget the moment the judge asked me if I was ready to meet the convicted felons. As soon as I said "Of course," the door opened and in entered a group of men and women in prison jumpsuits, ankle chains, and waist chains, and wearing flip-flops with socks. As they sat down and stared at me, the judge said sternly to the group, "Okay, everyone, this is Matt. He wrote the book, so Matt go ahead and share."

I was frozen. I had never seen another human being in chains before. It literally broke my heart. I was at a complete loss for words. But something told me that the best thing I could do was to let these men and women know how much they mattered. I'm not sure of the exact words I used during my fifteen-minute pep talk, but it was clearly effective. I was just trying to give them hope. After I finished, one of the convicted felons stood up and said, "No one ever told me that I mattered; that's why I ended up where I am today." With that, I watched a six-foot-six, three-hundred-pound man break down in tears.

This convicted felon changed Every Monday Matters, the company, and me forever. He showed me that I still had it all wrong. For me, EMM was still all about the numbers. What if, because of EMM, we could prove that there is less litter, more volunteers, less this, more that? For example, one of the Mondays in the book is: "Don't Flick Your Cigarette Butt." In writing the book, I learned that every year in America we smoke 300 billion cigarettes. Even worse, we litter 100 billion of those cigarette butts every year. I measured a cigarette butt and figured out that if you connect every one of those 100 billion cigarette butts end to end, they would span from L.A. to N.Y.C. 337 times a year. So we basically build a cigarette-butt freeway across our country every year. And we argue whether or not or why we have environmental issues in the world. Sorry, I digress. My thought was, what if, because of EMM, we could get that number down to 90 billion? Or 80 billion? What if we could change the numbers?

But this convicted felon, a man whose name I don't know and whom I will probably never see again, changed how I see it. Yes, litter is an environmental tragedy, but this convicted felon taught me that the biggest tragedy is that every single person who littered one of those 100 billion cigarette butts didn't think it mattered. They also didn't believe that they themselves mattered. In other words, our environmental problems are really just human problems. And the same with any other problem we see in the world. So change the way people see themselves and help them connect with how powerful they are, then we can change the world. In other words, we change the world from the inside out. Mind blown.

With this new understanding, I decided to transition Every Monday Matters from a for-profit company to a not-for-profit organization. I don't own it anymore; I just work there now. There's no ownership or equity in not-for-profits. Our mission is to create a world where everyone knows how much and why they matter. We launched a brand-new education program that now serves over 2 million students nationwide. We continue our work with companies to help them create workplace cultures where people feel like they matter. We are launching a senior program that will be rolled out in assisted-living communities to help our seniors reconnect with how much they matter in the last part of their lives. And last year, ten years after my first book came out, I wrote my second one, *Every Monday*

Matters: How to Kick Your Week Off with Passion, Purpose, and Positivity. And now comes this, the book that I have always wanted to write. Somehow, some way, my breakdown has become a blessing, and I wouldn't have changed a thing about it.

As I sit here and type these words on the page, I realize that everything I have gone through over the past nearly twenty years—the good, the bad, and the ugly—was to bring me to this book, *You Matter.* This book is different. It goes deeper. It's more personal. I realized that before my breakdown, I lived a pretty easy life. Sure, I had bad days. Sure, I've had my heart broken and have lost friends, pets, and family members. But for the most part my emotions lived on the positive and bright side of things. If we put our emotions on a continuum, with "As Good as It Gets" on the far left and "As Bad as It Could Be" on the far right, I might have only experienced about 75 percent of that spectrum, leaving out the final 25 percent to the right.

But that one Monday morning changed everything. Now I know what resides in that remaining 25 percent. Now I know what despair, helplessness, and hopelessness feel like. Now I understand how people can consider taking their own lives. Fortunately, I didn't. But experiencing those emotions has given me a new understanding of what it means to be human. It has changed the way I see people, for if it could happen to me, it could happen to anyone. On paper, my life looked great. Deep inside it couldn't have been any different. It has gifted me a deep sense of empathy and compassion for people that I never had before, because I never want anyone to experience what I did . . . yet I know it's possible they are experiencing something similar, or have before.

I know I created Every Monday Matters. I wrote the books, I started the company, and now the not-for-profit. But in a beautiful Frankenstein-ian sort of way, Every Monday Matters has also created me. It has made me a better and more complete person. It has challenged me and inspired me. As much as I am asked to come inspire others, the stories of the people I have met along this journey have inspired and changed me tenfold.

This book is not only a chance to share my story, but, more important, the stories of other people and the incredible teachings I learned from them. I am committed to helping you fully embrace how much and why you matter, and I believe this book will do just that. Because, whether you know it or not, you matter to yourself. You matter to your family. To your friends. Your company. Your community. Every word you speak. Every thought you have. Every action you take matters. It's time for you to truly love yourself for who you really are. You matter.

WARNING: CHANGE HAPPENS HERE

Taking a journey like this is never easy. It takes work. It took each of us some time to get to the place we are currently in, so it might take a minute to unpack our junk, implement some new tools, and transform ourselves and our lives. To help, I have organized this book around three fresh perspectives that will provide a new framework for how to live your life. Each of these perspectives is paramount to living a life that matters, and you will find yourself weaving in and out of them throughout your days ahead, always mindful of where you are at any given time.

Before getting into these perspectives, I also want to come clean about something. Yes, I know this book is entitled *You Matter.*, but you're also going to become super aware of and comfortable with the statement "It's not about you." I know, seems paradoxical: "I matter, but it's not about me." Trust me, it was strange for me to first hear that as well, but it is the very thing that changed my life. More on this later. I also know that you purchased it from the "Self-Help" section of the bookstore. Well, I am here to say that I think that "Self-Help" is only half of the conversation. We don't each live on our own private island of one. We are social creatures who live in a social context. So as much as this book is going to focus on the "inside" of you, it is also going to focus on the "outward" nature of you. For I believe that self- and social transformation are first cousins and they happen interchangeably at the same time. Stay with me; it will all make sense right now.

The book is divided into three sections to help move you through this self- and social transformation process:

• **"I Matter"**—The understanding of self. An opportunity to embrace your uniqueness and to be authentically you.

To embrace your inherent specialness. To know that you have agency to feel good about yourself, in all of your brokenness and imperfections, and to design a life that best honors your personal health and well-being.

• **"You Matter"**—The understanding of your ability to affect someone else. An opportunity to embrace how your actions, words, and thoughts play a significant role in how other people in your life feel about themselves and life in general. Maybe it is a family member, a coworker, a dear friend, or just someone you see occasionally as part of your typical routines.

• **"We Matter"**—The understanding of your connection to and ability to influence the larger fabric of humanity. This can be done either individually or with others. Either way, this is an opportunity to embrace how powerful you are in impacting total strangers, people on the fringe, and even people completely around the world, and how they will do the same to you. Life is a "we" thing, and you are part of something really big.

Shall we begin? There is a lot at stake here . . . in the best and most beautiful of ways.

I Matter

I am unique and one of a kind.

I am perfect and perfectly imperfect.

I am worthy and belong.

I am valued and valuable.

I am me.

I matter.

Be Authentic
SING YOUR SONG

Sing like no one's listening, love like
you've never been hurt, dance like
nobody's watching, and live like it's
heaven on earth.

—Mark Twain

I have been a swimmer most of my life. Actually, more
of a water polo player. I had the great fortune of playing
water polo for UCLA and coaching for two years after I
graduated. The good news about a sport like water polo is
that it pushes you to the greatest of your fitness and athletic abilities. The level of conditioning is hard to fathom,
and the physical rewards are pretty awesome. Trust me,
one day my wife, Patty, found one of my old water polo

pictures and stunningly looked at me and asked, "Babe, what happened?" Hence, the bad news about water polo: once you stop playing, you truly stop playing. It is not too often that you see a pickup game of water polo at a local pool. And every year, at our UCLA alumni game, those of us who have been retired from the game for several years certainly feel the pain and the embarrassment of putting on our Speedos, which clearly shrank in the wash. So now I just go with, "I'm a swimmer."

The cool part about swimming is that you can do it for the rest of your life. You can swim on your own. You can swim with friends. You can go as fast or as slow as you wish. It's just you, the lane lines, and that never-ending black stripe on the bottom of the pool. And, unlike places to play water polo, there are public pools all over the city that offer lap swimming, either as a pay-per-swim sort of thing or by joining a U.S. Masters Swimming program, for those overachievers.

I found my lap pool in West Hollywood, sandwiched between the modern and massive Pacific Design Center and West Hollywood Library. This little public pool is 25 yards long, with six swim lanes, old chipped lane lines and tiles, and a shallow end of 3 feet deep and a deep end of 15 feet. Tiny spill gutters mean the water stays a bit wavy. My guess is that it was built in the sixties, and in a very sweet and refreshing way, it hasn't changed much since.

Most of the new pools today scream "speed" and "competition." They're fifty meters long, with huge spill gutters, fifteen to twenty lanes, and fifteen feet deep at the shallowest. Modern. Cold. You know the ones. You see them on the Olympics every four years. Not "my" West Hollywood pool. It was OG.

Because of its community feel, my pool also attracts a certain type of swimmer. Sure, it has its West Hollywood Masters Team, but then there were us weekend warriors, and we created a texting group and, on any given Monday, Wednesday, or Friday, one of us would send out the "Who's in?" For eight years, at least three of us would answer "Me." This group of people became my friends. My community. We laughed together, pushed one another to work out harder, celebrated birthdays, and somehow became the Mötley Crüe of the WeHo Pool.

If I have learned one thing, especially as I have gotten older, it is the absolute need for community. When we were younger, community was built into our lives in the form of classrooms, schools, sports, clubs, family, church, and summer. However, as we graduate from some of these institutions or structures in our life, we slowly find our way out into the world, a bit disconnected and isolated. If you are twenty-two years old or older, my guess is that you have felt that void. Don't drift too far alone; community matters.

There was one other swimmer at our little community pool whom we never swam with but who left an indelible mark on all of us. His name is Chris. We never knew his last name or his age, but I would guess mid-twenties. He is African American, a bit overweight, and always came to the pool with his school backpack overstuffed with books. I will never forget his big eyes and smile and his warm greetings. And while we were always swimming in the two "fast lanes" in the center of the pool, Chris was by himself on the far-right side in the "handicapped lane."

One evening, while swimming, Chris yelled to me across the pool: "Hey, Matt, Matt, Matt, what is your phone number?" Keep in mind, we were both swimming and in the water at the time—no pen or paper or cell phone in hand. I responded with my number, and Chris simply replied, "Thank you."

The next day, I received a text from Chris. "Hey, Matt. It's your friend, Chris. We are friends, right?" I couldn't believe he remembered my number. In this day and age of just saving people's contact information in our phones and simply hitting "Call" or "Send," I didn't think anyone remembered numbers anymore. The truth is, I even forgot I gave it to him.

I quickly replied, "Hey, Chris. Of course we are friends; thanks for texting me."

Chris replied, "Good. Friends? Friends? Right?"

From that text exchange forward, Chris became one of my closest friends at the pool and proceeded to teach me so much about life. Chris is not autistic; rather, he *has* Autism. Big difference and a lifelong lesson that he explained to me. Just like someone isn't cancer, they *have* it.

The reason he remembered my number is that he is a math wizard and has a photographic memory. He loves numbers. He also loves people. Chris knew the name of every employee and every swimmer at the pool. He simply greeted them with, "Hi, I'm Chris. What's your name?

Can we be friends?" And from then on, every time he saw you, he would greet you with, "Hi, _____, friends, right?" I saw him do it over and over and over again. It was so brilliant and beautiful.

Chris and I continued to text each other for several years. He even called me from time to time, just to make sure we were still friends. Together, with the rest of our little swim team, Chris even created a team cheer. In childlike Chris fashion, it was pretty simple: "1-2-3, Wooooooooo!" The "1-2-3" part was paired with three high fives, to be immediately followed by the "Wooooooooo!"—at which time we would shake our heads, open our eyes big and bright, and put our hands up in the air, as if to show an explosion. We did this cheer at least five times every Monday, Wednesday, and Friday evenings, Chris always leading the charge and making sure he high-fived every single one of us at least once.

One evening I came home from the pool and Patty asked what was in my hair. I had no idea what she was seeing or talking about. Upon further investigation, she looked at me and said, "Babe, why do you have braids in your hair?" I smiled and said, "Chris put them in." She smiled, shook her head, and replied, "Of course he did." I also believe she secretly loved it, because she saw how much I cared for Chris, someone she would have loved to meet and care for just the same. She's sweet like that, just not quite as extraverted.

Besides being good at math and names and cheers, Chris was also a world-class hair braider. We are talking perfect cornrows in minutes. He could make them big or small and always asked what size first. For some reason, he picked me to be his first hair client at the pool, but that quickly spread to more of us. I even noticed that, eventually, Chris added a Ziploc bag of rubber bands to his backpack and was clearly ready for anyone. I can still hear him today: "Matt. Matt. Braid? What color? How many? More? More?" On any given evening, at least two of us would leave the pool with cornrows, and we loved it.

But of all the joy and kindness and gifts that Chris offered all of us at the WeHo Pool, there was one particular thing he did that moved me the most. He hummed and sang while he swam. Chris only knew one stroke, kind of. He would push off the wall on his back, wearing goggles the size of old pilot glasses, and slowly pull his way down the lane. It looked as though he was making snow angels the entire time, but somehow it propelled him, slowly, to the other end. And with every pull of his arms, he would sing. Always loud enough for all to hear, but never clear enough to recognize a single song.

But what I did recognize was his bliss, which is what I will never forget. In the moment, Chris didn't have a care in the world. He wasn't concerned with being judged. He might not have even been aware that we could hear him. It was just himself immersed in the moment, perfectly present, and authentically Chris.

It's been over three years since I have seen Chris or heard from him. Most of us have moved and don't live near the pool anymore, and our Mötley Crüe has disbanded. But I often wonder if Chris is still there, singing and snow-angeling along, doing a team cheer with a new group of swimmers, and hopefully braiding some new heads of hair. I used to tell Patty, and it is something that I still think about today: "I wish I had more Chris in me."

See, Chris is one of the most authentic people I have ever met. He is unabashedly himself. Every day. In every moment. Just Chris. There is no judgment of others or himself. No pretense. No agenda. No facade. No filters. With all of his "imperfections," he just steps into life and connects people. Even with his limited verbal skills, he is able to bring people together like nothing I have ever seen before.

So what is holding us back? Why can't we just be our authentic selves, without judgment, and stop posting a fake version of our lives and ourselves on social media? Why can't we just show up every day as our genuine selves? Who are we trying to prove something to, and why?

I believe it is because many of us don't feel like we matter. Instead, we are insecure. Living a life alone in our own heads, exhausted and unable to connect with one another or our true selves. We are constantly performing as if we are actors on a stage, playing characters believable enough to others but not genuinely ourselves. I did it for years in the music industry. I had a title, and that title carried with it certain expectations, not always the most righteous. My friend Andrew used to say to me, "You are your costume."

What he meant by this is that my work attire brought with it certain behaviors and shifts in my personality, compared to my weekend attire or uniform or costume. My work costume was disingenuous to myself and to others. And this truth is exactly why, after years of healing, my therapist finally said to me, "You know, Matt, the first day you walked into my office, you were just a shell of a person. You were completely hollow and disconnected from your true self."

This is not the life we are meant to live. This is empty. Fake. Utterly consumed with what other people think of us. It is also why we struggle with empathy and compassion in our lives and in the world. For starters, we would rather judge someone instead of walk in their shoes for just a few yards. Judging is much easier to do than taking the time to invest in others, to learn their stories, and to understand why they might be different from us. But this is also a self-fulfilling prophecy: for the more we judge others, the more we believe others must be doing the same thing to us. So we have created this false fear of always being judged, which only pulls us away from our authentic selves. Sorry, women, you really have this down to an art.

But this is why singing like no one is listening, and dancing like nobody is watching is so important. Because God forbid we dance and sing while someone is watching. We would make fools out of ourselves and look less-than or dorky or ugly. Well, Chris would say, "Swim and sing like everyone is watching . . . especially when they are." Because that's what he did, and that's what we all need to start doing. Get ready to lose your voice.

TAKE ACTION

Pick one song that will, starting today, be your official song. Pick a song that uplifts you, inspires you, gives you energy. Download it. Put it on every device you have. Memorize every single word of it. Even feel free to put dance moves to it. Then sing the crap out of it—at home, in your car, at your desk, while hiking or walking the dog. This is YOUR song. From this point on, see yourself as the person who wrote it, then commit to singing it at least once a day, especially when someone is watching. (Heck, if you really get inspired, make a whole playlist of songs that lift you up and make you happy!) And, while you're at it, just start showing up a little bit more as your true self. Trust me, it will feel amazing, and no one is judging you. The truth is that, if anything, others will notice how much more fun and meaningful it is to be around you, which just might lead to new friends. Interesting how that happens . . . just ask Chris.

JOURNAL PROMPT

Get super honest with yourself. In your journal, write down this question:

What is it that holds me back from being my true and authentic self?

Take a breath and then identify what the thing holding you back is and how it shows up in different parts of your life. Then write it down. You might even discover that there are different things that keep you from being your authentic self in different parts of your life. For instance, maybe your work reason is different from your personal life reason. Once you've identified it (or them), write it/them down with specific detail. Then use a "5-Whys" strategy, asking yourself "Why?" five times for each of your reasons. For example, if you wrote down, "I'm afraid of speaking my truth," then ask yourself "Why?" You might answer, "Because I am afraid of rejection." Then ask yourself "Why?" again. After five "whys" you will most likely see that none of it really makes sense and that confidently speaking your truth is a whole lot easier.

CONVERSATION STARTER

You have been asked to pick a theme song for your grand entrance at an event. What song would you pick and why? Just make sure to pick one that you can confidently sing and hum in front of everyone as you enter.

2

Be Wise
KNOW WHAT
MATTERS MOST

Every morning we are born again. What
we do today is what matters most.

—Buddha

In 2014, I was asked to be a presenter at TEDxYouth in San Diego, California. Meaning I was going to be speaking in front of five hundred high school leaders, mostly from California. Tough audience. Trust me.

It's commonly known that public speaking is considered our number-one fear. If you are like me and most other people, you can relate. Somehow, the years of doing it have helped me become fairly comfortable with it, even when I'm sharing my personal story, which as you now know, wasn't always so pretty. But TED events are different. They carry gravitas, a pressure that everyone feels, from the presenters to the production crew to the volunteers to the audience members. It's as if everyone knows that something special is supposed to happen or else it is a complete failure. I have had the pleasure of feeling that pressure a few times, and it never seems to get easier. So much so that I believe if our greatest fear is public speaking, then our *even greater* greatest fear is actually public speaking at a TED event.

To prepare for my talk, I sent out a survey to high school leaders across the country and asked them to answer two simple questions:

QUESTION 1:

Tell me how you think other students at your school would rank these fifteen items, from most important to least important:

1. Going to prom

2. Getting good grades

3. Being an athlete or a cheerleader

4. Having the nicest new gadgets

5. Going to college

6. Being best looking

7. Being most popular

8. Having the largest social media following

9. Making a difference in my school or community

10. Being a good friend

11. Being in student government

12. Having a boyfriend or girlfriend

13. Getting a good SAT score

14. Being healthy

15. Being a role model

QUESTION 2:

Imagine that CNN called you and invited you to give a one-hour speech to the entire country about high school students today. What would you want the American audience to know about you as a group?

The answers I received told a story that I believe all of us should learn from and can relate to. Let me start with Question 2. The students said things like:

"We might be different from you, but that doesn't make us bad."

"Believe in us; we will be the generation that finds the cure for cancer."

"All we want is to feel like we are heard and that you see us."

"One day we will create the greatest world we have ever seen."

I heard hope in their answers. I heard a future president. I was inspired to know that the future looks bright for many years to come. Well, I felt this way until I read the answers for Question 1. Remember, their answers to the first question were not what they personally thought; rather, they were what they thought the majority of students at their school would say. Here were their top-five most important items:

1. Being best looking

2. Being most popular

3. Being an athlete or a cheerleader

4. Having the largest social media following

5. Having the nicest new gadgets

Quite a different picture than the one painted by their CNN address answers. In fact, I'm not sure if there could be any larger a contradiction. How is it possible that these are the five top priorities of the generation that will bring us the greatest world we have ever seen? Even more telling and confusing was which item received the most number-fifteen votes. You guessed it: "Making a difference in my school or community." Ouch. Something didn't add up.

I believe that these answers would be pretty similar if I

had asked the same questions to adults and they answered them honestly. I know that is not easy to hear, but I think it is true. We would say that we want to make a difference in our community, yet most research shows that only one in five Americans volunteer and that they spend thirty-two hours a year doing so. At the same time, nearly half of adults spend an average of eleven hours per day consuming media in the form of TV, radio, computers, smartphones, internet, and tablets. We also want to stay young and attractive, and we spend a fortune on it. We want to be popular and known for something, often using social media as a way to feel seen or famous. We are obsessed with sharing photos of our new car and our always-perfect vacation on Facebook and Instagram. We even use filters to make everything look that much better. We trade in our perfectly good cell phones every two years to get the newest model, even though we know our environment pays the price. Starting to make sense?

I don't say this to be judgmental toward others, because I am not immune either. So much of my career in the music industry was driven by the same forces. I wanted nice things. I wanted to be known and on the red carpet at VIP Hollywood events. I wanted to be fit and spent outrageous amounts of money on gyms and trainers. And, of course, I wanted that house on the hills—the Hollywood Hills, no less. Why? Because this is what I thought mattered. This is what I thought being successful was all about. This is what I thought would bring me joy and purpose and meaning. And all it took was a massive panic attack and some deep depression and severe anxiety to show me that I had it all wrong.

But let me be careful here, because I honestly don't think there is anything wrong with being wildly financially successful, being popular, having nice things, or being attractive. Not at all. I say, "Go for all of that and more." But I also want to be bold and honest enough to let you know that none of this is why you matter. You matter because you are unique. You matter because you are a gift to the world. You matter because you are one in some eight billion. You matter because you are a mom, a dad, a brother, a sister. You matter because you belong here.

The problem is that we have placed all of our value on the wrong things, and we are suffering from it. I call it "Fool's Gold." And it has all of us mesmerized and scrambling for answers. But we will never find them here, because this is not what matters, yet this is how we spend all of our time and energy.

I also believe it is why we feel the massive divide in our culture today. In a desperate search for mattering, too many of us are choosing everything that doesn't matter, and we end up with realities that don't serve our greater good. I matter because I am the president. I matter because I'm going to be known by pulling off a mass shooting. I matter because I am a gang member. I matter because my religion is the only one. I matter because of where I live. I matter because of my gender. I matter because of my sexuality. I matter because of my race. I matter because of my political party. I matter because I have wealth, power, pride, ego.

The list goes on and on, and we, as a culture, are all losing, because none of this is why we were put here on earth.

This is also why people say to never have conversations about religion or politics. So many of us have made our political party or religion what matters most to us. I'm sorry, but you don't matter because you are a Republican or Democrat, so stop letting that lead your choices. You matter for something much bigger than that.

Whenever my work gets overwhelming, when the news on TV breaks my heart, or I just feel like something is slightly off, I turn to these two quotes, which I have printed and framed on my desk, to recenter myself. I hope they inspire you the way they do me:

What Will Matter

Ready or not, some day it will all come to an end.

There will be no sunrises, no minutes, hours or days.

All the things you collected, whether treasured or forgotten, will pass to someone else.

Your wealth, fame and temporal power will shrivel to irrelevance.

It will not matter what you owned or what you were owed.

Your grudges, resentments, frustrations and jealousies will finally disappear.

So too, your hopes, ambitions, plans and to-do lists will expire.

The wins and losses that once seemed so important will
fade away.

It won't matter where you came from or what side of
the tracks you lived on at the end.

It won't matter whether you were beautiful or brilliant.

Even your gender and skin color will be irrelevant.

So what will matter? How will the value of your days
be measured?

What will matter is not what you bought but what you
built, not what you got but what you gave.

What will matter is not your success but your significance.

What will matter is not what you learned but what you
taught.

What will matter is every act of integrity, compassion,
courage or sacrifice that enriched, empowered or
encouraged others to emulate your example.

What will matter is not your competence but your
character.

What will matter is not how many people you knew, but
how many will feel a lasting loss when you're gone.

What will matter is not your memories but the memories of those who loved you.

What will matter is how long you will be remembered,
by whom and for what.

Living a life that matters doesn't happen by accident.

It's not a matter of circumstances but of choice.

Choose to live a life that matters.

—Michael Josephson

Success

To laugh often and much;

To win respect of intelligent people and the affection of
     children;

To earn the appreciation of honest critics and endure
     the betrayal of false friends;

To appreciate beauty, to find the best in others;

To leave the world a bit better, whether by a healthy
     child, a garden patch or a redeemed social
     condition;

To know even one life has breathed easier because you
     have lived.

This is to have succeeded.

—Ralph Waldo Emerson

So what matters most to you? The answer might surprise you. What matters most to you is what you spend most of your time and resources on. Are you spending most of your time and resources on things that bring you joy and feel authentically "you"? Maybe you are in perfect alignment already and are truly living a life that matters per the poems I shared. But chances are, since you are reading this book, maybe you now realize that your life needs some adjustments, your priorities need some shifting. Not that you are doing anything bad or wrong, but you just aren't spending enough time on what truly matters to you. Make this your opportunity to truly connect with why you matter and to begin living a life consistent with that. And protect it with all of your heart.

Know that people might judge you. Trust me. People in my life started to notice my different choices and priorities and they didn't like it. They liked "Party Matt," not "Litter-Picker-Upper Matt." But ultimately, they didn't like it because I just became a mirror for their own lives, and sometimes a little self-awareness is tough to accept. You can trust me on that as well. But set your new boundaries and get used to saying no to things that don't align with what matters most to you. For this is your life. This is your time. And time spent on what matters most is never wasted time.

TAKE ACTION

Spending time on What Matters Most should not sound like punishment or that life can no longer be fun. It's quite the opposite, because the rewards are far greater and more meaningful. Joy is greater than fun. Gratitude is greater than happiness. Deep connections are greater than followers. Significance is greater than success. Purpose is greater than pleasure. So pick one of the above feelings—joy, gratitude, connection, significance, or purpose—and make a plan to bring more of it into your life. Here are some ideas to help you, but certainly go with whatever comes to your mind and heart: Joy—Start a new hobby. Gratitude—Journal every day. Connection—Designate a specific time for relationships. Significance—Volunteer and be of service. Purpose—Write out a mission or purpose statement for your life. Of course, you can choose to do all of these as well. But just do it.

Time to create your "What Matters Most" pizza. That's right—write out a list of everything that matters most to you. Once you have your list, then draw a big circle in your journal and make a slice for each item on your list and label each slice. Starting from the center of the pizza, color in each slice of pizza based on your own self-assessment of how well you are performing for each item. For example, if you wrote down "health," but you aren't exercising on a regular basis, you aren't eating well, or getting enough rest, your "health" slice might not get colored in too much. But don't worry and don't judge yourself for it. . . . This is all about making changes and embracing how much you matter. Once you have completed your pizza, take note of where you need some improvements and commit to doing at least one thing in each slice to take it to the next level. It's going to feel so good.

What is one super-meaningful part of your life that you wish you spent more time on? What changes can you make in order to achieve this? What changes will you commit to right now?

Be You
YOU'RE NOT A MISFIT

Be yourself; everyone else is already taken.

—Oscar Wilde

In every family there is a "Golden Child." You know, the one that can do nothing wrong and just sits there with a smirk on his or her face while their siblings get scolded. My brother, Michael, earned that 24-karat-gold title in our family. I love and adore my brother. He is the smartest, sweetest person and just an overall amazing human being. But, damn it, I just wish he had done one thing wrong. Straight A's his entire life, never caught partying past curfew, photographic memory, 99.9 percent on every standardized test he ever took, classically trained acoustic guitar player, Stanford undergrad, UCLA medical school, UC Davis Residency Program. Now he is a chief of medicine for a major health-care company, married with two beautiful children, two labradoodles, and a brand-new stunning home that they just built. He's never even had a frickin' cavity.

How could I compete with that? Well, I couldn't. And I didn't. Maybe you can relate to this. Or maybe you were the Golden Child and don't feel like you ever lived up to the expectations you or other people placed on you. Gotta love that performance pressure.

For me, it was the former. As a kid, I wore green and yellow Pumas to my first day of kindergarten and have never stopped wearing bright and crazy tennis shoes to this day. From sticking a vitamin C too far up my nose, to eating my grandmother's heart pills, to biting through my tongue while eating a carrot, to getting bit by a brown recluse spider, I have taken up permanent residence in emergency rooms across the country.

One day a woman walked up to my mom at the grocery store when I was just four years old to compliment my mom on her beautiful child. My mom sweetly responded, "Thank you, this is my baby, Matthew," to which I interjected, "I am not a baby, thtupid." Yes, S's were hard for me. Embarrassed and brokenhearted, my mom started crying and immediately left the store with her full cart sitting in the aisle.

On a different day, my mom asked me and my friend to stay in the car while she ran into her friend's house to grab something. As my luck would have it, one minute later a guy rode up on his bicycle and said, "Hey, you want some candy? See that motor home over there? There are huge bags of candy behind it." Being the "Un–Golden Child" that I was, my best friend, Michael, and I hopped out of the car and made our way over to the motor home only to discover that there wasn't any candy there at all. When my mom came out of her friend's house, I shared the story with her because I was upset that this boy on his bike lied to us. My mom, eyes wide opened, yelled, "Matthew, where is my purse? There was a big check in there." Her purse was gone. See what I mean? Definitely not the Golden Child.

In some ways, things got better as I "grew up." Well, maybe only a little better. I mastered the ability of the annual car accident. When I worked as a bank teller during one of my high school summers, I rarely balanced my drawer at the end of the day. And the summer I sold Shasta soda for three months, I also totaled my company car.

My college years went fairly smoothly, but postcollege got a bit dicey. As I shared before, finding my path in life wasn't the easiest. My first job out of school was with M&M/Mars, where I became a candy sales rep. People were thrilled. Great pay. Great benefits. I even got a company car—a metallic blue Ford Taurus station wagon. My friends called it my "Chick Magnet Mobile." Nothing like going from playing water polo for UCLA to driving a station wagon with M&M and Snickers decals on it in about two weeks' time. Over a year and a half, I gained forty pounds because I ate fast food for lunch and candy for snacks. After my second Halloween season I decided selling candy was not my life's calling, so I quit. My five-and-a-half-year streak of parental good graces was about to end as well.

My father worked in sales for a large consumer-brands company for forty-seven years. He supported our family on it and did very well for himself and for us. My brother, as you now know, went into the medical field, and there are only two of us children in the family. My mom's dream was to have four boys, but she stopped with two. Yours truly. And the truth is that if I were the first, I might have been the only. And when the son who was "supposed to" follow in his father's footsteps quit after eighteen months what his father did for forty-seven years, you can guarantee the "father-son" conversations were back in season.

"Dad, I know I walked away from a good opportunity, but I knew that was not the career path for me," I explained. "I just need to find myself still." I know that I am not unique this way. I have met so many people, young and old, who are still looking for themselves. And, as if that's not hard enough, they then need to figure out how to make a living. For the lucky ones, they have aligned the two. For most of us, we haven't, and we live disconnected lives—work and life.

The next few years were just that . . . trying to find my career and myself, and doing my best to narrow the gap between the two. I taught after-school programs for a year but quit when I realized that most of my students were not very good swimmers or didn't have the joy of water that I had. For some reason I figured I was the person to change that, so I started Pollywog Aquatics, a private swim-lessons company in L.A.

In Los Angeles, there is a little neighborhood called "Beverly Hills." I am guessing you are familiar with it. I don't remember how this all started, but somehow I became the private swim instructor for families in Beverly Hills. It was awesome. I would show up at a house—or mansion—hop in the pool in the morning, and every thirty minutes they would bring me a new kid to teach. Somehow these families had an incredible number of cousins, so I ran the every-thirty-minutes-a-new-cousin program. I was hooked, but not everyone else was as convinced.

"Dad, listen, they pay me cash, I'm supertan, I play Marco Polo every day, I get to hang out in big beautiful homes, and the moms all hit on me because their husbands are absent," I pleaded. Nope. Didn't work . . . again.

At this point, I had to stop fighting it. "If you can't beat it, join it," so they say. I figured medicine worked for my older "Golden Child" brother, so maybe it would work for me, too. Well, my medical career lasted one day. After taking the courses to become a certified emergency medical technician, I was welcomed to the realities of the job and survived one of the most stressful and disgusting days of my life while on my first ride-along. I was out. The good news of that one-day career, however, was that I learned enough to drive myself to the doctor that dreadful Monday morning. Or maybe that was just my *Starsky & Hutch* moment in life.

Once again I felt like that little boy searching for candy that was never behind the motor home.

Out of options and tired of letting people down, I decided to go back to school. I attended the Anderson School of Management at UCLA in 1995 to pursue my master of business administration (MBA) degree. My plan was to expose myself to something new—a new industry, career path, plan for my future.

On the second day of orientation, we all had to take the Myers-Briggs personality test. If you are not familiar, the test is based on Carl Jung's and Isabel Briggs Myers's approach to personality typing. The test is a series of sixty-four questions that, once completed, classifies you with a personality type based on four letters.

There are sixteen different Myers-Briggs combinations and they are organized in a chart for comparison purposes. Not to oversimplify this test, but at the opposite end of the scale of an "ESFJ" is the "ENTJ." An ENTJ is "very leadership-oriented. Likely to be top executives, business persons. Big on reducing inefficiency, ineffectiveness. Take-charge people. Can be overwhelming to less outgoing types." In short, ESFJs are considered "Most Harmonizing," while ENTJs are considered "Most Commanding."

As you imagine these sixteen unique personality types on a scale again, basically draw a line in the middle, with eight types on each side of the scale with ESFJ farthest to the left and ENTJ farthest to the right. In my section of sixty students, fifty-nine of them were to the right of the middle line. Not only were they right of the line, but they were in the farthest right quartile (25 percent) and decile (10 percent), with the majority of them actually being ENTJs. Makes sense, right? This is a top business school in the country, so the description fits to a T, "Leadership-oriented. Likely to be top executives." But there was that one remaining student who wasn't on the right side of the scale at all. And, not only was he on the left side of the centerline, but he was as far left as one could go. The lone ESFJ. Me.

During the orientation of a two-year program, I already felt like I didn't belong. The test proved it. It wasn't even something to argue. I was an ESFJ in a world of ENTJs. Did I make another mistake in my life by going to business school? Once again, the questions were flying my way. I was still searching to find myself in the world but feeling like a permanent resident on the "Island of Misfit Toys" in the old *Rudolph the Red-Nosed Reindeer* cartoon movie. Can you relate?

*   *   *

I have spent most of my life trying to fit in, wanting to belong. To fit into the structures placed in front of me and to live a "normal" life. Part of it was driven by my fear of being alone. Part of it was living up to expectations, both my own and the subtle ones placed on me. Part of it was just trying to navigate being human.

I believe these are fairly natural motivations for people. The problem, however, is that we often lose ourselves in our pursuit of fitting in. Instead of better understanding ourselves and embracing our uniqueness, we try to mold ourselves into something we are not, all in the name of fitting in. We start living as people pleasers, always trying to win the adoration and acceptance of others, while forgetting to love and adore ourselves. And as we disconnect from ourselves, we open the door to anxiety and depression. If it gets bad enough, we might become easy pickings for online porn, alcohol, drugs, religion gone bad, gangs, terrorist groups, and more. *Maybe these activities or people will make me feel good again and finally give me a sense of mattering.* No, they won't.

A few years ago, I had lunch with a friend who asked me if I ever saw myself as a "diamond in the rough." I pondered quickly and said, "No, that's not something that ever crossed my mind," and the conversation shifted. As I was driving back to my office, I called my mom and dad just to check in, and I shared Heather's question with them. My mom started chuckling and said, "You know, Matthew, during our parent-teacher meeting with your first-grade teacher, she asked us whether or not we knew our son was a diamond in the rough."

It all finally clicked for me. It was time for me to stop trying to be part of the rough. Someone saw that in me when I was just seven years old, and now at fifty years old. And, most important, I finally saw it. I was not a misfit toy. I was just "ME." An ESFJ and so many other things that make me "ME." Even the things that I used to judge as mistakes or bad choices, I now embrace because they happened and because they are "ME." And I wouldn't change it for the world.

What about you? How much of your life have you spent trying to fit in or belong? Just taking the path of status quo because that is just what people do? Go to school, get good grades, go to college, get a good job, get married, have kids, work until you retire, then call it a day . . . or a life. I bought into that life plan for my entire life—right up until I realized that it wasn't the plan I was meant to be on. But because I thought I was, it created immense anxiety in me. Why? Because it always made me feel like a failure. Like an outcast. And it created internal tension and control issues for me. It created doubts and "Woulda, Shoulda, Coulda's." My soul kept saying, "It's okay, just go be you," but my head kept saying, "Get your life together like everyone else you graduated from business school with." This cognitive dissonance nearly killed me, and I know I am not alone.

We need to remember that our world thrives on diversity, color, and uniqueness. Don't believe me? Then picture the opposite for a moment. How about a world where everyone is exactly the same—the same size, color, hair, eyes, thoughts, tastes, likes, dislikes, movements, emotions, and personalities. Sure, you would fit in just fine, because you would literally be a clone of everyone else. But isn't that one of the most uncomfortable and horrific realities to consider? Both you and the world need you to just be "YOU."

Let's stop trying to force ourselves to be someone or something we are not. Just be you, not some story that you have made up in your mind or a story that you think you are supposed to live. I thought I was going to be married at twenty-eight, have three children by my mid-thirties, be a multimillionaire by forty, and retire at fifty. Instead, I got married at forty-three, have no kids, I founded and run a not-for-profit organization, and I am now fifty and not even close to retiring. But the best part about it is that I have never been more fulfilled and aligned than ever before in my life. I am finally unapologetically "ME." Don't you think it's time for you to finally be unapologetically "YOU"?

TAKE ACTION

A brand-new diamond was just discovered—the rarest of all diamonds. You have been asked to write a description of this one-of-a-kind wonder with the goal of selling the diamond to the highest bidder. Remember that effective sales copy is loaded with adjectives to really grab the attention of potential customers. Even more effective sales copy focuses on the benefits someone will experience by purchasing and owning a product. But here is the deal: in this case, *you* are the diamond. So what makes *you* so unique, special, and rare? And how does the world or your family or how do your friends or colleagues benefit from having you in their lives? Because they do. Happy writing.

JOURNAL PROMPT

What is one thing about yourself that you always thought made you different in a bad way? Maybe it is something physical, like a mole on your face, freckles, an injury, a stutter, or too much of something or not enough of something else? Maybe it is something more mental or emotional, like a fear of something, a feeling of inadequacy, or the story of your past or upbringing.

Pick one of these things and write it a love letter or a poem. Make sure it knows how madly in love you are with it and that you wouldn't have changed anything about it, even for a second. I can hear it now: "Dear Nose." "Dear Being Different." Have fun with it, but really think and feel it through. When you are done with your love letter, have the courage to share it with someone. This will help you truly shift it to a more positive and healthy place. Whomever or whatever you decide to write to, please thank it for me, too. I love it because it made you just the way you are today. It matters, too.

Was there ever a time in your life that you didn't feel like you fit in? What was the scenario, and how did it make you feel? Did it eventually get better? If so, how and why?

Be Perfect
COMPLIMENT YOURSELF

I now see how owning our story and
loving ourselves through that process is
the bravest thing that we will ever do.

—Brené Brown

Many of us live life completely wiped out. We wake up tired
and we go to bed just the same. For some, it's because of
our work. Maybe we live life on the road—either as a freeway commuter or traveler from airports to hotel rooms
and back to airports. Or maybe our work is in the service
industry, like in schools, hospitals, assisted-living communities, juvenile halls, or nonprofit organizations, and we
spend the entire day serving others. And if it isn't work, it
could be from personal reasons, like being a mom or dad,

having a sick and aging parent, or simply not taking proper care of our health. Regardless of how we get there, the fact is that it's really challenging to connect with how much we matter when our bowls are empty and we have nothing more to give. We have been served out and are in desperate need of being served.

A few years ago, I led a training for a group of about forty after-school educators to boost morale—to help each of them know how much they mattered to themselves, their students, their schools, and their communities. After about an hour into the training, I gave each of the educators a black silicon wristband that had the words YOU MATTER on it and asked them to partner up with someone in the room for a simple activity. Once paired off, I explained that I wanted them to spend a few minutes sharing how much they appreciate one another, but they had to step out of the "work" stuff, so "I really appreciate the fact that you are always on time for work" wasn't going to cut the mustard. Instead, I wanted them to get more personal and touch on their person's essence, character, and heart. Then at the end of sharing a few heartfelt words with one another, they could exchange their wristbands and simply say, "You matter to me," before slipping on their wristbands.

I love watching this activity because it challenges people to have to look up and see one another. It's something we did more effortlessly before smartphones, social media, and the internet became a part of our lives, but our ability to connect with one another, especially face-to-face, has been on a steady decline. While this activity is awkward at first for people, something shifts, almost like riding a bike again for the first time in twenty years, and the muscle memory comes back and our ability to connect starts to shine through. This is when the magic happens.

I scanned the room, carefully taking mental notes on each of the pairs as they exchanged their comments and wristbands. I saw smiles and laughter. I saw hugs and high fives. Possibly most telling of all, I saw a lot of tears and people wiping their cheeks and eyes. After a few minutes, I brought the group back together and simply asked them if they enjoyed the experience.

Their replies were amazing: "It felt so good to stop for a moment to take the proper time to acknowledge my partner. . . ." "We have become so bad at really seeing one another, so it was nice and refreshing. . . ." "I guess I really needed that, based on how emotional it made me. . . ."

Seeing that they were moved, I then asked them the big question: "Was it easier to say these nice things to your partner, or was it easier to hear your partner say them to you?" It was unanimous: "It's easier to say them than to hear them."

What would you have said? I believe this is a telltale sign that we are not doing well, both individually and collectively. In our opinion, we are the most dominant and advanced species in the universe or any other universe, for that matter. In the twenty-first century, we have become so advanced that we are not comfortable with people giving us compliments. It's as if we have to do everything in our power to deflect, devalue, or distract from the awkwardness of the moment. I've done it myself. I will never forget the time someone told me they liked my jacket, and I instantly replied, "I like yours, too," only to discover they weren't even wearing one. Maybe something similar has happened to you.

The problem with our inability to embrace compliments is that we are running out of ways to connect with one another. We know bullying is a bad thing, for we don't like it when people put each other down, either in person, in the press, or on social media. Simply stated, the opposite of bullying would be lifting one another up—complimenting one another—and we just determined that this isn't so comfy, either. So what's left? Indifference. Let's just stop even acknowledging one another. I see it in line at the grocery store while everyone stares at their cell phones and no one connects with one another. I see it in restaurants while moms and dads finger through their social media posts, completely ignoring one another and their two-year-old-child in the high chair.

A culture of indifference is a lonely, disconnected, sick reality. There is nothing human about it. For our world and ourselves, we must learn to embrace compliments. Not only do we need them for our own self-esteem and confidence, but also the sooner each of us learns to embrace and receive compliments, the sooner we will be better at giving them. After all, if something makes us uncomfortable, why would we do it to someone else? We wouldn't, and that's part of the problem.

*   *   *

Flustered by the group's response, I instantly came up with
an idea and asked them to pull out a piece of paper and a
pen. I explained that I was going to give them one minute to write down five things they do or did well. To help
them, I shared that these could be specific things, like "I
made an awesome dinner last night for my wife" or "I ex-
ercised really hard this week." Or they could be something
more general, like "I am a good listener" or "I love to make
people smile."

I quickly shouted, "You get one minute. Go."

As the group was writing, or at least trying to write
down their five things, I slowly made my way around the
room to check in. Some of them had written down three
things. Some were stuck on one or two. All of them looked
a bit perplexed and were scratching and clawing for things
to write down.

After a minute, I yelled, "Stop. Put your pencils down."
I hated when my teachers yelled that after a test when I was
a child, so I guess it was my way of getting back at them. I
clearly have issues, too.

I congratulated the room on what seemed to be a challenging exercise for them and then asked them to stand
up with their lists in hand. I also shared that they could
spread out a little bit to have some room and personal space,
because they might want it.

Then I gave them one more minute to compliment
themselves out loud for everything they wrote down on

their lists, but they had to say their first names before each of their compliments. In other words, "Jill, you did an amazing job at running two miles this weekend." "Jill, you are always such a good friend." "Jill, that pasta last night was incredible." "Jill . . ." Once they made it through their lists, they had to start over until the minute was up.

The looks on their faces were priceless. To lighten the mood, I joked that if they only wrote down one thing they do or did well, they were going to sound like a parrot for the next minute. I also warned that I expected them to be loud and proud, or I would add time to the minute.

"Go!" I cheered, and started the clock.

I was a little worried, because I didn't know what would unfold during this second minute. I had never done this before. But my nerves quickly settled as the compliments got louder and louder. They were having a blast—laughing, dancing, even high-fiving each other. It was hilarious but also obviously meaningful.

I stopped the group after one minute and asked, "Besides really awkward, how did that feel?" They laughed and glowingly shared how much fun it was and that they were really glad we did the activity. But then something happened that caught the entire room off guard. Helen, a woman toward the back of the room, raised her hand and said, "This was one of the most challenging things I have ever done. I didn't even write down one thing I do well."

There was a collective sound of sadness and shock in the air, for Helen's fellow educators obviously think she is amazing and couldn't believe that she couldn't think of a single thing she does well. I was also shocked, because literally ten minutes before we started the wristband exchange, the LCD projector in the room stopped working and Helen was the one who ran out to get us a replacement. She literally saved the day just moments prior, but she didn't include that on her list. Nor did she include that she shapes the lives of our youth, which she has been doing for nearly thirty years.

I looked at her deep, sad eyes and asked her if she was okay. She nodded without saying a word. She was too emotional to get one out. Then I asked if we could help her fill in her list of five things. Helen looked down for a moment and then looked up with tears streaming down her face and said, "I have been in an abusive marriage for twenty-six years and have not heard a compliment in all twenty-six of those years. I only get told how poorly I do everything, so I don't even know what a compliment is anymore." She bowed her head into her hands and was overcome with sadness.

With emotions running high and a deafening silence in the room, I told the group to take a ten-minute break. I needed to pull Helen aside to make sure she was okay, but I never got the opportunity. As soon as the word "break" came out of my mouth, Helen was instantly showered with love. Not a single person stepped out for the break. They only stepped in to make sure Helen knew how special she is. Some of her colleagues hugged her. Some of them gave her compliments. A small group of them even started a list for Helen with way more than just five items on it. All I could do was stand and watch one of the most loving gestures I have ever seen.

For that moment, and possibly for the first time in twenty-six years, Helen knew just how much she mattered.

Sometimes our feelings of "not good enough" and "not worthy enough" are the result of our life experiences. It might be something in the media that makes us believe we have to look perfect. It might be a parent who makes us only feel seen or heard when we perform and accomplish at a level high enough for them to feel proud to share at cocktail parties. And sometimes it might be a spouse, like in Helen's situation. And if outside influences aren't enough, sometimes our feelings can be self-inflicted.

Well, I have news for you, and I hope you hear it loud and clear and take it deeply to heart: You are already perfect, so stop pursuing perfection. You are one in nearly eight billion. You are a unique gift and blessing to the world. For it is your very existence that makes the world what it is today. Love yourself. Compliment yourself. Just say "Thank you" when someone else compliments you, and soak it in for a moment. You deserve it. Because you matter.

I promise you that you have an endless list of things you do or did well. Give yourself one minute, or even an hour, and write them down. Keep a running list while you are at it. And, of course, don't forget to compliment yourself and everyone around you on a regular basis. Compliments heal. Compliments spread joy. Compliments can change the world.

"You matter."

Please just say, "Thank you. I know I do."

Now we are getting somewhere.

TAKE ACTION

I wasn't joking. Pull out a piece of paper, a pen, and your stopwatch and write down five or more things that you do well. Then stand up and read them aloud (remember to put your name at the start of each one) for another minute. And then congratulate yourself for not only being willing to do this exercise but for actually doing it. You can do this by yourself or with friends, family members, or colleagues.

JOURNAL PROMPT

Based on your "Take Action" experience, set aside time to journal about it. How many items did you write down? How did the experience feel for you? Take more time to add to your list and even ask people in your life for help. Don't worry about what they will think. Just explain that you are doing this "project" and need outside perspectives.

Note: If you are really struggling with this experience, please consider talking to a professional. Trust me, there is nothing wrong with getting a life coach. I believe that every single person alive should have one. But the bottom line is that you have so much to offer and do so many things well, and I want to make sure you embrace that about yourself. You need to know, and the world needs you.

CONVERSATION STARTER

Why do you think it is so challenging for people to accept compliments? How can we change this?

5

Be Bold
MAKE A STATEMENT

You are both a work of art and an artist
at work.

—Erwin McManus

As we move into the final chapter of the "I Matter" section, I think it's important to stop for a minute to reflect. I know I have been coming from a place of believing that you matter simply because you are you. That, by your very nature, you are special. This idea that your existence gives you an inherent "mattering" might be challenging to accept, for it seems to ignore or devalue your life experiences and how those might have shaped how you feel about yourself in this very moment or in general. Each chapter of our story can easily detach us and distract us from our true essence—this pure desire to be good, to do good, and to feel good.

My friend David founded and runs one of the most successful branding and advertising agencies in the world, and he has an activity that he calls "Netflix." He doesn't mean the company Netflix; he means something different. Well, kind of. The core premise is that we all easily get caught up in our own little movies of life—that before we know it, we have spent our entire lives deep inside each movie or chapter of our life, never mindful of the bigger picture or our bigger self. Instead, he says, "Just be Netflix." In other words, step outside of each movie of your life and see yourself as something bigger. Know that you are Netflix and that these movies of your life are just stories. Part of your larger catalog. So watch them and enjoy them, even when they don't feel good or aren't fun to watch, then go back to being Netflix. Awe. I love this, but I can also hear you saying right now, "If only it were that easy."

I hear you. Because your stories are real. Your emotions are real. Believing that you have inherent value that only you can bring to this world is not always easy to embrace.

At the same time, there are also people who would say they are still connected to that inherent sense of significance and mattering, but I would argue that the majority of them are mistaken, as each one has forgotten his or her true essence. Their significance is tied to materialism and ego. Again, this is why I thought I mattered. It was all about success and performance and titles. But that is not why we were brought into this life. The intention was far more important than that. But whether you have just lost touch with your inherent mattering or you have attached to the wrong things, there is still the opportunity to transform.

This is why this chapter is so important, as it illustrates the interconnectedness of the "I Matter" and the "You Matter." Because sometimes, like I did, we will begin to connect with how much we matter internally when we start to connect externally.

I am not sure why, but for men, going to the bathroom is not a group or a friend thing. It is a solo operation, meant to be performed quickly and quietly. I can't recall a single instance where I heard a guy say to another guy, "Hey, I have to use the restroom; you want to come with me?"

Now, for women, it's a completely different story. Using the restroom is a joint effort, a true social experience. I imagine that being in the women's restroom at a public location is filled with conversation, laughter, a little bit of gossip, and a whole lot of shared mirror time. The men's room, on the other hand, might as well be a library. No talking. No eye contact. Minimal mirror time. Just get in and get out. And, of course, be cool.

Following an event at which I had just spoken in Las Vegas, I needed to use the restroom. Now, if you have ever been to Vegas, you know that everything they do is over the top. The clubs, the casinos, the shows, you name it. Vegas spares no expense, and this policy also applies to the public restrooms in their grand casinos.

As I walked into the men's room, I immediately noticed the sound of my soles tapping on the tan marble floors. As I gazed up, I marveled at the tan marble walls and countertops, the crystal chandeliers, and the gold fixtures. So rococo, dare I say "cheesy." I also noticed that I was the only person in the restroom. Realizing this was actually a bit strange, given there were around twenty urinals on the wall and five stalls. In other words, this restroom was built for traffic, but in that moment, it was my very own personal Versailles.

Since I was alone, this gave me options, and I had to make a big decision. I didn't want to pick the very first urinal, because that one is probably the most used and least pristine. Also, if someone else came in, there was a good chance they would pick the second or third one, simply because they wouldn't have to walk as far. I wasn't in the mood to be shoulder to shoulder with someone, so I walked about two-thirds of the way down to, say, urinal number twelve, if they were numbered. I felt great about my choice.

As I was preparing to do what a guy does at the urinal, I heard a familiar sound—footsteps tapping on the tan marble floors coming from the front door. My private bathroom castle was no longer just mine. But in the spirit of being cool, I just looked straight ahead as if I never heard or saw a thing.

Apparently my bathroom intruder also needed to use a urinal, and his pick of the urinal litter was the one right next to me. That's right, urinal number eleven. Of all the choices, he had to become my neighbor. At this point, a lot of unspoken social norms kick into play. You have to act as though you are falling madly in love with the tile right in front of your face . . . staring deeply into its eyes. Then there is the "90 Degree Rule"—you don't look down or left or right past 90 Degrees. As the silence loudens, you then have to ponder whether or not to say hello or to just ignore. And, if it all falls apart, you can always just wrap things up even if you haven't started what you came there to do in the first place.

As I was processing all of the options, my intruder made it clear that he had made up his mind already. He wanted to start a conversation with me.

He said, "You know, you taught me something."

In that moment, all hope of relieving myself quickly flew out the door of my personal mansion. As I stood there, frozen, staring at the wall, I thought, "What on earth could I have taught this total stranger that I have never met or even looked at?" But I also knew there was no escaping now, so I hesitantly asked, "Oh, and how is that?"

He answered, "For all of my life, I had it that I needed to learn how to love myself before I could love anyone else, but you showed me that by loving other people, I can actually learn to love myself."

Ah . . . my intruder had actually heard my message, and it had an impact on him. So much so that he felt compelled to share it with me in the restroom. And in that exhale moment, my intruder suddenly became my friend and relief actually happened.

*   *   *

I don't know that I will ever have a public restroom experience like that again. But I can't deny the significance of what my intruder shared and the conversation that followed. I believe that this concept about love is both life- and world-changing. I witnessed it with my new bathroom buddy, and I have experienced it myself. The challenge is that we live in a "Self-Help" and "Me, Me, Me" world. We think that the arrows always have to be pointing inward. What can I get? How can I feel better? What will this mean for me? All it has done is leave us numbingly narcissistic. Part of this is because we have bought into the idea that *the more I get, the more I get.* It's become our culture. And it has left most of us feeling alone, empty, and not loving ourselves.

But the other part of this is that we also believe what my bathroom buddy believed: *until I love myself, I can't love other people.* For the lucky ones, they are able to love themselves with ease and have developed a sense of acceptance and awareness for who they are and what they have to offer. Those folks didn't need the last five chapters of this book. But for many of us, we struggle. We question why we matter. We beat ourselves up more than we love ourselves, and all this does is keep us from loving other people or letting other people love us. This only leads us to further isolation, depression, and not living our most honest and truthful lives.

I had the pleasure of meeting an amazing woman

named Jennifer, who is one of the greatest examples of how this "I Matter" and "You Matter" dynamic works. Jennifer was a successful trial attorney and partner at one of the most prestigious law firms in the country. Her three brothers were all extremely successful businessmen, and all of the four siblings were married, had children, and were thriving in life.

One day, Jennifer and I were having coffee and talking about life and she shared with me that she was on the board of a nonprofit organization whose mission is to end the cycle of homelessness for children and families in Orange County, California. I learned that day that Orange County has over twenty-eight thousand homeless children in its public school system. Yes, in one of the wealthiest counties in America. Jennifer explained to me that Project Hope Alliance was in the process of looking for a new CEO/executive director and that some of her board members thought she should take the job. She clearly wanted my opinion.

The first thing that came to mind was that there was no way she could take that big of a pay cut, for she had a family and financial obligations and had built a lifestyle around her and her husband's combined income. Plus, she had worked so hard to create her career and she would have to give up everything she'd accomplished, not to mention undertake a major downsizing of her life. But then Jennifer shared with me that, besides the income, there was one other major concern: Jennifer and her brothers and parents had spent much of their life homeless, and this was not public knowledge. They had been a "motel" family, like so many families today.

I was in utter disbelief, but I immediately knew one thing: Jennifer needed to take that job. I started sharing more about my story. I talked about my breakdown. I talked about starting my organization. And I talked about downsizing my life and walking away from a career because I knew my story could help people. And I vividly remember saying to her, "You know, a $5 Footlong from Subway for lunch and another one for dinner isn't all that bad."

Today, and for the past five years, Jennifer Friend has been the CEO of Project Hope Alliance. She has moved over one thousand children and families out of homelessness, supported hundreds of kids through high school graduation into college, and has taken the organization to levels it had never seen before or imagined. Jennifer was selected to be part of the Clinton Global Initiative, among other accolades, and she has told her story on stages across the country.

Jennifer and I recently had lunch together, and she said, "Matt, thank you for helping me understand that my story was never about me. I was always so ashamed of it. I spent so much time and energy trying to hide who I was, and this continued into my adulthood. But you gave me the courage to embrace my story and to share it, and that has changed the lives of so many people, including my own."

As my eyes watered up, she said one more thing that

cracked me up: "You know, Matt, as soon as you mentioned your meals from Subway, I knew that if you could do it, so could I. As long as my family had food, who cared about the rest of it? It was just stuff. And my desire for stuff will never be greater than my desire to make a difference and to live out God's calling on my life."

The blessings that have come from her sharing her story are far more profound than her old fears about what sharing it might do to her life. It's no longer about her; it's about the thousand-plus lives that have been changed. She has found her true self by sharing her true story, even when she struggled with loving it herself, and now lives are forever changed . . . including hers.

Yes, we each matter, but maybe it's not always about us. Let's dig into this deeper next, in the "You Matter" section.

TAKE ACTION

Pull out two Post-it Notes and write each of these statements on them:

> "I need to learn how to love myself before I can love somebody else."
> "By loving someone else, I learn to love myself."

Stick them on a wall, your bathroom mirror, computer monitor, car dashboard, or wherever you will see them. Then place one more, blank Post-it Note below each of them. On each of the blank notes, write down three ways you are going to put the statement above it into action in your life. In other words, three ways you are going to love yourself more and three ways you are going to love others more. Then take action to make those things happen.

JOURNAL PROMPT

Once you have accomplished all six of your actions on the notes, pick one experience from loving yourself and one from loving other people and write about each one. How did each experience make you feel? Was one more challenging than the other? Was one more powerful than the other? Really connect with how you felt in each scenario. Then write a promise statement to yourself, that you commit to continually taking action to love yourself and others more often. And, just for fun, imagine if that was how every single person in the world started their day. Let's make it happen . . . starting with you.

CONVERSATION STARTER

Do you think it is easier to love yourself or to love other people? Why?

PART TWO

You Matter

Your words have impact.

Your presence is felt.

Your creativity inspires.

Your actions speak loudly.

Your powers are super.

You matter.

Be Super
SHOW YOU CARE

> Nobody cares how much you know,
> until they know how much you care.
>
> —Theodore Roosevelt

We have lost one of the most powerful ways of connecting with one another and letting someone else know how much they matter to you. Yes, even a total stranger. It's called, "The Art of Asking Questions." It is such a simple tool to show someone you care, but it doesn't mean we use it enough. It is also how we get to know one another on a deeper level. How do these questions make you feel, and when is the last time someone asked them of you?

How are you?

How is your family?

What are your hopes for the week?

If you could go on vacation right now, where would you go?

How are things at work? At home?

How did you meet your significant other?

What do you love to do in your free time?

If you could have one wish, what would it be?

What is your greatest fear?

What is your greatest accomplishment?

Even as I typed these questions, I am imagining you, and I would love nothing more than to hear your answers. With these ten questions alone, I would have such a sense of who you are. I also imagine that you would think I truly cared about you . . . or why else would I be asking? Right? Fortunately, for me, I learned the importance of asking questions from a high school student . . . even though I was forty years old at the time.

As I pulled into the parking lot of a high school in San Diego, California, my heart was heavy and my nerves were at full attention. Everything was gray—the cement of the parking lot, the paint on the walls, the clouded-over sky. It certainly wasn't the first time I was asked to visit a school to inspire students, so that was nothing to feel uncomfortable about. In fact, I have probably done over one hundred school assemblies. But for some reason something felt different this day.

As I entered the auditorium, I was greeted by a large group of students and educators. After being introduced, I walked up to the microphone stand and looked out at all of these young faces. I didn't say a word. I just looked. It was almost as if I was searching for something. Some sort of cue or clue or answer to this overwhelming feeling that something needed to change. Then it came to me.

I opened with, "Okay, everyone, I know I was supposed to come down here today to talk to you, but I think today is a good day for 'us' to listen and for 'you' to talk, so I am turning the microphone over to you. This is our day to learn from you . . . to get to know you. What makes you happy? What struggles do you have? What do you like about school? What don't you like? What inspires you? What scares you?"

In the middle of uttering this grand plan of mine, I quickly noticed the shifting and discomfort of all of the educators in the room. I could even hear their thoughts: "Oh no, where is this going?" "What will the kids say if they get the mic?" "Are we sure this is a good idea?" In some small way, the "Oh crap" look on their faces assured me that I was doing the right thing and that we were on the verge of something special. At least, that's how I had to see it, since there was no turning back. I was creating space for the room to join me.

Things started slowly. Some of the students just looked straight down. Others were looking at one another and waving their brows, almost to say, "You go." Clearly, the students didn't know if it was okay to be honest and vulnerable, not just in front of one another, but also in front of the staff. But I continued to let them know that this time and space was sacred and safe. That in order for us to serve them best, we needed to get to know them better.

And then it started. One brave boy slowly walked to the microphone and shared that he never felt like he fit in to any of the many cliques on campus. His honesty and vulnerability gave the other kids permission to talk, as we sat and listened to one topic after another—gangs, bullying, drugs in the bathrooms, homelessness, not feeling respected or appreciated, and so on. At times it was hard to hear. At times it felt hopeful. At times we held our breath, and other times we exhaled. While it was only an hour, it felt like it needed an entire day. It was a privilege to enter into an open, honest conversation about real experiences and humanity with our current generation. By the time I pulled out of that parking lot, my heart lifted and my nerves settled down, and I knew something magical had just transpired.

I couldn't remember my two-hour drive back to Los Angeles. Not a single on- or off-ramp or even a street sign. Not a passing car. I didn't even have my radio on or my phone in my lap. I might as well have been driving on Mars, because Lord knows where my head was. I guess I was processing what had just taken place.

What happened next is straight out of the California Lottery commercial: something along the lines of "It was a day just like any other . . . until it wasn't." As I walked into my house, my phone dinged because I received an email. It read, "Hi, my name is Nikki. You just came to my school and allowed us to share. You made me feel like I was important, and I needed that because I am homeless."

My heart stopped. Nikki. I remember her so clearly. She was a beautiful girl with big eyes and a huge smile. I remember how she sheepishly approached the microphone and shared that there was a homelessness issue at their school. But I didn't know that she was homeless herself. How did she have the courage and strength to do this? I wondered if anyone else knew she was homeless. So much for my calm heart.

I immediately shifted into my we-have-to-do-something-stat mode and called the educator who organized my visit. During the conversation I learned more about Nikki, but I also learned that this high school had over one hundred homeless students. I was dumbfounded and made plans to come back to the school as soon as possible.

When I went back to visit with Nikki and her after-school teacher, Anya, she shared a story that no one ever wants to hear about a young girl. Nikki had been burned, prostituted, stabbed, raped, and impregnated—a childhood from hell and she had the scars to show for it, both internally and externally. For Nikki, being homeless was better than being "home." And so she went out into the world without a roof over her head or food to eat. Scared and scarred.

Hearing her story broke my heart and enraged me, all

at the same time. How is it possible that someone could do such a thing to this beautiful young girl? I guess in some ways I didn't want to believe that stories like this truly exist. That it just isn't possible for people to be so wicked and cruel and literally do all they can to ruin someone else's life. Maybe I was just naïve and too utopistic. But what I do know is that for Nikki, and for me, everything was about to change.

As I sat in the room with her, I don't think Nikki really believed I was actually there again. The mere fact that I took the time to drive back down to San Diego to spend time with her was almost more than she could handle. At times she was beaming. Confident. Filled with hopes and dreams and fully receiving the love we were giving her. Then, at other times, she broke out in severe episodes of the hiccups. Rapid fire—thirty at a time. I had never seen anything like it. In response to the perplexed look on my face, she said, "I often hiccup when I start to feel uncomfortable. It's a nervous tic sort of thing." It was as if, at certain times, her insecurities and lack of trust or self-worth kicked in, and me being there was too much. Too kind. Too sweet. Too foreign.

I quickly felt like I was in over my head. I was not a trained therapist or social worker. I wasn't an expert in domestic abuse and proper protocols, reporting, or counseling. But I did offer what I could: my heart. More than anything else, I wanted Nikki to feel loved, knowing that it might be the first time she had ever felt it. And together we created a plan that day to shower Nikki with love.

Anya welcomed Nikki into their home. Nikki and I talked on the phone at least once a week, and I included her in programs at my company and introduced her to my friends and family. We laughed. We cried. We listened and coached, when she invited it. And before she knew it, Nikki was surrounded by a community of people that loved her unconditionally. That was our gift to her. Love heals. And Nikki healed us, too. Together, we proudly watched Nikki, with those big eyes and even bigger smile, walk across the stage to receive her high school diploma just two years later. A moment I will never forget.

We all love a good story. Even when we know the typical story arch and how the story is most likely going to end, we still can't look away. We read or watch as we fall in love with the main character, and we journey with him or her through trials and tribulations while reaching for their hopes and dreams. Nine out of ten times the hopes and dreams come true, yet we sit on our stools of pins and needles until that special moment happens. Phew. Then we do it all over again with the next story.

A lot of great stories also commonly offer three types of characters—the villain, the victim, and the hero. Think about any Marvel blockbuster or *Star Wars* film, episodes of *Game of Thrones* or *Outlander,* or timeless books of fiction, like *The Lord of the Rings* or *Harry Potter.* If they are really good, they even have a way of connecting us to each of the characters—yes, even the villain at times. A villain doesn't often become the hero for us, unless his name is Robin Hood, but a villain often becomes the victim, because at some point in time each one might have been a victim before becoming a villain.

But what happens when we apply this model to our own lives? After all, we each have a story. Now imagine your story is the next great novel or blockbuster movie. Would it be a story about a villain? Someone who goes through life putting people down, disregarding anything good or positive, committing crimes (maybe of the heart, not necessarily breaking the law)? Or would it be a story about a victim? Someone who is always on the short end of the stick because it is always "someone else's fault" or doing? Someone whom "no one cares about," "never gets a fair chance," and needs the world to cry them another river? Or would it be a story about a hero? Someone who goes through life leaving a positive impact on the people and places he or she encounters? Someone who looks for opportunities to lift people up and do the right thing, and stands as a beacon of hope and goodness in the world?

I am not here to judge anyone, because I have played all of these characters at some point in my own story. But what I know now is that only heroes can see the extraordinary in the ordinary and are fully committed to serving others, to connect, to be authentic and aware, and to be willing to change and overcome their fears. Heroes bring their unique superpowers to positively impact everything around them.

Admittedly, we are human. We can't jump over tall buildings, stop speeding locomotives, shoot webs out of our hands, or fly with just a cape. Sure, it is fun to imagine, and I have always loved wondering what superpower I'd have if I could choose. For the record, mine would be to don my special cape and fly on my own. Road rage, be gone. But while we are mere humans, this does not mean we don't have superpowers. Maybe your superpower is that you make people laugh. Maybe you are a great hugger. Or maybe you cook amazing meals and bring people together around the dinner table. Or maybe you drive back to San Diego to show a homeless teen some love. Or maybe you do all of these and even more. Because I believe that each of us has limitless superpowers, and we often don't even realize we are yielding them.

So what about you? Have you ever considered yourself a superhero with superpowers? Have you really thought how powerful you are and how profoundly you impact your surroundings, either intentionally or unintentionally? Because one thing I know is that you are a ripple-effect machine. Everything you think, say, and do ripples out and impacts those around you. And, not to sound creepy or make you uncomfortable, but you should know that somebody is always watching. Think about it: you watch people's behaviors all the time . . . and their behaviors impact you. How did you feel when you saw a customer get rude with the server at a restaurant or the salesperson in a store? On the flip side, how did you feel when you saw a person helping someone with disabilities cross the street? I know you felt something. Whether you like it or know it or not, people feel certain ways based on your actions, too.

Knowing this brings intention and greater meaning to our actions. As Gandhi once said, "A nation's culture resides in the hearts and in the soul of its people." In other words, every day we wake up, we have a very personal question to ask ourselves: Am I going to be a positive or negative influence on the world today?—because I am one of the authors of our culture. If we want more love in our culture, then let's be more loving. If we want more gratitude, then let's be more grateful. The same goes for tolerance, friendships, mindfulness, selflessness, joy, hope, compassion, and anything else we hold important in our hearts and souls. And it is our superpowers that will make all of these realities and will create the life and the culture we all want to enjoy.

Several years ago, I was invited to lead a give-back experience for a big pharma company in San Francisco, California. Many organizations had gotten a little tired of rope courses and scavenger hunts for their team-building experiences and they were looking for something more impactful. To help me create the experience, I reached out to some people who lived in the area. I know San Francisco pretty well, but having that local finger on the pulse is always helpful. I also connected with a student from the College of the Redwoods, a few hours north of San Francisco, and together we designed a powerful way for the eighty employees at this off-site retreat to support the homeless population in the city. We had our plan and knew it was going to be a special day.

Before our big day began, we had a team meeting to make sure we had everything in place and had checked every last detail off of our prep list. We were ready to go with hours to spare, so I recommended going for a little walk just to get some fresh air and enjoy the beautiful scenery.

After following the trail for about thirty minutes and huffing and puffing our way up the final hill, we were rewarded with one of the most majestic views looking south over the Golden Gate Bridge, with the San Francisco Bay and the city right behind it. We stood there silently for about five minutes, just soaking in the sun, the wind, the sounds, and the sights. It was sensory overload in the most beautiful of ways. Then I broke the silence and asked, "Can you believe we are here? Look at this view. And now we get to go inspire a group of eighty people and help them make a difference in the lives of homeless men, women, and children. Did you ever imagine?"

Nikki turned to me and smiled. "When I was fifteen, I didn't even think I would make it to eighteen, let alone be able to inspire someone else. But when you came to our high school in San Diego that day, I saw you as a "Professional Superhero." You came into my life and made me feel important. Like somebody truly loved me and saw that I was capable of creating something special with my life. That was the first time I have ever felt that. And to me, that was your superpower. And once you shared your power with me, I became a superhero myself, with the same superpower that you had . . . the power to lift people up. So, now I am a professional superhero as well."

Thank God I asked . . . every single time.

P.S.: Nikki didn't leave a dry eye in the room that afternoon. A professional superhero at work.

TAKE ACTION

Think of five people in your daily life, then write down five questions that you want to ask each of them. You might ask each of them the same questions, or have specific questions for each of them. Totally your call. Once you have your people and their questions, ask away. Enjoy connecting with them and discovering more about them, potentially even their superpowers. Also, take close note of how it makes them feel. Don't be surprised if they ask you, "Why are you asking me these questions?" The truth is, they are probably not used to it . . . which is all the more proof and reason we need for doing it. Nice work helping them know how much they each matter to you.

JOURNAL PROMPT

You are a superhero with superpowers. The world is ready and waiting. Are you? Write a story about yourself as a superhero. What would your power be and how would you use it to help other people connect with how much they matter? Remember, the story can still have challenges, but at the end you are back on top and impacting everyone around you.

CONVERSATION STARTER

If you could have one superpower, what would it be and why? Keep in mind: it doesn't have to be something fictional or superhuman.

Be Aware
LOOK AROUND

Attention is the rarest and purest form of generosity.

—Simone Weil

I go to my local Starbucks every morning when I am not traveling. The strange part of this routine is that I don't even drink coffee. Sure, I love their green iced tea and a few of their breakfast sandwiches, but I wouldn't say they are enough of a reason for me to get in my car first thing in the morning to head to Starbucks. Surely I could make breakfast and iced tea at home, but that would take away something in my life that I need dearly. Community.

Yes, I go to Starbucks every morning to see my friends. I don't order via their app in order to get in and out as quickly as possible. And my Starbucks doesn't have a drive-through window. Both the app-order pickup area and the drive-through would defeat the purpose. I want connection, which requires me to stand in line, sit down, wait for my order, and actually have conversations with people. If I haven't freaked you out enough already, I also don't look at my phone while waiting. I look up, take note, hold the door open for people, and, yes, make friends.

A few years ago, Patty and I moved to a new part of L.A., so I needed to establish my new favorite Starbucks. As you can imagine, L.A. has a Starbucks on almost every corner, so the options are plenty. After factoring in all of the important criteria, I settled on a Starbucks in a little shopping center with plenty of parking and a real community feel. It was the perfect fit.

Much like the first day of school or the first day at a new job, getting acclimated and feeling part of the current culture can take a moment. For me, it might not take as long, because I tend to engage people fairly quickly, but it is still a tad foreign, and I was a new customer at this particular location.

In a matter of weeks, I knew most of the morning baristas and they knew me. Most of them, especially the good ones, even remembered my order, and I started to feel at home again. So much so that after just a few months "inside," I found myself buying each of them $25 Amazon gift cards for the holidays. BFFs now.

In addition to the staff, I started seeing some of the same customers as well. This particular Starbucks had a nice sitting area with four brown leather couches in the corner. I quickly observed that every morning was like an episode of *Cheers*. The same four guys in their same respective seats . . . every morning. The best part is that none of them came in together. Nor did they know one another before making this particular Starbucks their watering hole. They were Starbucks friends.

Over time, I got to know each of them. I appreciated all of them, but it was David that intrigued me the most. He was always the most welcoming to everyone. He smiled. He waved. He pulled people's chairs out for them. He single-handedly changed the energy in the room. Even better, he did this without saying a single word, because David is deaf.

David and I clicked instantly. His desire to spread joy and kindness was so contagious and something I have always strived for myself. Because of David, I started watching ASL (American Sign Language) videos on YouTube. Because of David, I started to look forward to going to my new Starbucks every morning. Because of David, I learned the importance of looking up and seeing the world around me.

I recently had a meeting on Balboa Island, a quaint island in the Newport Beach marina in Orange County, California. You can only access the tiny island via ferry or by driving over a small stone arched bridge. Balboa is famous for its narrow streets lined with immaculate gardens and multimillion-dollar beach "cottages." You can't visit the island without enjoying a chocolate-dipped frozen banana, walking along the waterfront, or simply watching people as they ride by on their bikes or in their sweet road-ready golf carts, small lapdog in tow.

Artyn and Max, the couple hosting the meeting, live at the far end of the island from the stone bridge, so I slowly navigated my way down Park Ave. Driving only 10 mph, it's easy to take notice of your surroundings. I chuckled as I passed Coral Avenue, then Sapphire, Diamond, Ruby, and Turquoise. They clearly had a theme going on. I marveled at the perfect front-yard gardens, seemingly maintained on a daily basis. And it would be a bit dishonest if I didn't mention the daydreams I was having of living in a few of the homes I drove by. This street was a far cry from the jam-packed ten-lane freeway I had just navigated for nearly two hours to get here, and I was blissfully enjoying my stroll . . . right up until the moment a dog walked in front of my car.

Jolted out of my bliss, I slammed on my breaks and barely missed the little dog. Heart racing, yet grateful, I just stopped in the middle of the road and watched this little dog slowly make his way out from in front of my car and across the intersection. He looked like a Cavalier King Charles spaniel, maybe twelve years old or so, and he was in absolutely zero hurry at all.

Once he was safely on the sidewalk, I looked around to

see if any potential owners were walking along as well, but I didn't see anyone. Clearly this dog was not supposed to be out, so I decided to investigate further.

Knowing I only had ten minutes before my meeting started, I needed to work quickly. I pulled over, parked my car, and set out to find the dog. It didn't take me long to catch up to him—again, he looked a little older and was taking his sweet time. As I approached him, making the universal dog clicking sound with my mouth, he stopped walking and turned his head to look up at me. In that moment, I understood why he walked right in front of my car: he was missing his left eye. He truly never saw my car.

I gently picked him up and cautiously looked at the tag on his collar. It gave a phone number and an address. The problem was that I was on Turquoise and this puppy lived on Ruby, a few blocks away. He was small and sweet enough, so I decided to just carry him home. Oh, and his name was Bear.

I knocked on the front door and no one answered. I then rang the doorbell, again to no answer. Finally, I poked my head over the side gate and yelled, "Is anyone home?" Again, no answer. At this point, my meeting was only a few minutes from starting, so I had to make a decision. I opened the side gate and started walking along the side of the house, which opened up into a courtyard type of area. Just as I noticed a water bowl on the ground and was thinking I could leave him there, another dog came out of nowhere and started barking and running toward me. Bear got a little uneasy in my arms, which made me think this wasn't the correct house, so I quickly back-pedaled toward the gate, staring down the other dog the whole time. Getting bitten by a dog was not supposed to be part of this rescue mission. Right as I was shutting the gate, with Bear out of harm's way, I noticed that the dog running and barking at us was missing a leg. Okay, how in the hell am I carrying a one-eyed dog, and a three-legged dog is chasing me and ready to take one of my legs?

Leaving Bear with the angry three-legged dog was clearly not an option, so I went to plan B and dialed the phone number on the dog tag. I typed in the number: 949-649-2357, then I hit "Call." As soon as I hit the "Call" button, a name popped up in my phone: "Jeff Miller." What? I have this one-eyed dog's frickin' phone number in my phone? This can't be possible. Is this Jeff Miller's dog? I haven't seen Jeff in over twenty-five years, since college.

No one answered my call, and there wasn't a personal-ized outgoing message, so as soon as the computer voice finished its commands, I said: "Hey, my name is Matthew Emerzian, and I think I found your one-eyed dog, Bear. Please call me as soon as you can." I didn't address Jeff di-rectly because I wondered if maybe that was no longer his number and now someone else had it.

Then I waited a few minutes.

And a few more.

And no one called me back.

At that point, I looked at Bear and said, "Well buddy, looks like you are coming to my meeting." Bear and I walked the few blocks back to my car, I put him on my lap, and we drove the remaining few minutes to Artyn and Max's home.

Artyn saw me walking up their front walkway holding Bear, so she immediately came outside to greet us. "Matt, why do you have this dog?" All I could do was laugh and share the story with her. Then Artyn, being the sweet angel on the earth that she is, said, "Well, bring Bear inside and let's get him some water."

As our meeting was wrapping up, I was trying to figure out what to do next. I couldn't stay on Balboa Island all day. I knew Patty would love Bear, so if I brought him home she would never want to let him go. But I also knew I had to find Bear's owner.

Then, just as I was packing my bag, my phone started ringing. "Jeff Miller." I answered, "Is this Jeff Miller, the person I went to college with twenty-five years ago?" He responded, "Yes, but Emerzian, why the hell do you have my dog?" We both laughed while I told him the story, which ended with me asking if I could meet him at his house to take Bear back. Jeff replied, "I would love to, but I am in Hawaii on vacation, and I have a buddy watching my dogs. Do you mind driving Bear back and taking him in through the side gate?" I replied, "Not at all," then I paused before saying, "Wait, does your other dog only have three legs?"

Sure enough, that was Jeff's other dog, and he was simply protective of the house and bothered by the fact that I was carrying his brother. Finally, the one-eyed dog and the three-legged dog were happily reunited. Oh, and the back gate was properly shut and locked, and hopefully Jeff now has a new dogsitter.

David recently turned seventy-five years old, and he and his wife invited Patty and me to his birthday party. We were completely honored yet also unsure of what a birthday party for a deaf seventy-five-year-old man would look like.

When we arrived at the restaurant, David immediately greeted us and walked us over to some of his friends. Then he took us to a new group and another new group. Such a gracious host, almost as if he was proud to let everyone there know we were friends. Besides feeling instantly welcome, it also became clear that this was going to be an experience like none other for us, because everyone there was also deaf. We smiled a ton. We hugged total strangers. We did our best to use hand gestures and facial expressions. And we hoped for a lot of lip readers in the room.

It was definitely a unique experience, but it was also so eye-opening. To begin with, we never stopped "talking" with people. It was so social, and everyone was so excited to be there. It was also the first time we have been in a room with forty people and not a single one was looking at a cell phone. There weren't even phones on the table during the meal. Again, something I have not seen in years. Instead, they all looked up and saw one another. Maybe it is because they had to, because that's how they communicated, but it was beautiful to observe. True relationships. True conversations. True community.

After we ate, David's best friend walked up to a little makeshift staging area to give a speech, in sign language, about David's life story. Thankfully they had a translator there so we could understand the speech and ultimately learn more about David's seventy-five years. At the end of his speech, his friend asked if anyone would like to share a few words about David. It was crickets, which is a bit of strange word choice, being that it was a birthday party where nearly everyone was deaf. But it was clear that no one was going to step up to share, until all of a sudden Patty waved her arms in the air and said, "Matthew has something to say." Before I could even react, she was sliding out of our booth so I could get out and head up to the stage. Nothing like your wife throwing you under the bus. I had to step up. See, as much as she makes fun of me for getting into situations like this, she secretly likes it and finds great humor in it.

To be clear, I don't know sign language. I have also never spoken with a translator. Plus, most of the people in the room have known David for decades, and I have only known him for three years. But I knew enough about him to share a few words that would help him know how much he matters to me and to the world.

I shared with the people in the room how much I enjoy starting my day with David at Starbucks. I talked about how much of a bright light he is and how he greets everyone with so much love and acceptance. And then I looked directly at David to let him know how grateful I am for our friendship. David's eyes started to tear up, as did mine.

Two people living completely different lives, challenged by communication styles, yet bonded by our deep desire for people to feel good, our love for life, and our shared desire to be friends.

As I was wrapping up my comments, it dawned on me that I also had a story I could share. The problem is that the story involved some R-rated content, and I didn't know anyone in the room, so I wasn't sure I should share it. But I decided to go for it.

See, when David and I were first becoming friends, it was a fairly quick exchange—a smile, a fist bump, a thumbs-up or -down, a wave. Occasionally, we would sit and write a few notes on Starbucks napkins, but the conversations were fairly shallow. In other words, there was still so much we didn't know about one another, including our personalities and our senses of humor.

One morning, while still in our initial friendship courting phase, I was waiting in a bit of a long line at the counter and David walked into the store. Now, the front door and the line for the cashier are at opposite ends of the store, so there was a good forty feet between us. We quickly made eye contact, and I waved, then David put the palm of his right hand on the forearm of his left arm, right near his elbow joint, and then flexed his left arm up toward his shoulder, as if doing a bicep curl. In other words, David just gave me the "Up yours" gesture, smiling the entire time.

I know he wasn't serious, but I also didn't know we were at that point in our relationship yet. Regardless, I decided to go along with him, and I put my hand in the air and flipped him off. Yes, smiling the entire time as well. David's facial expressions changed quickly, and he put his hands out to his sides as to say, "Why are you flipping me off?" So, of course, I did it again . . . smiling.

After placing my order, I walked over to his table and sat down chuckling. It was somewhat cool to me that David and I had already reached that fun, healthy, trash-talking stage. Then David pulled out a napkin to write something on it. Before showing me what he wrote, he repeated his same "Up yours" gesture with his arms and then pointed to the napkin. The napkin read "Good Morning!"

David was simply saying "Good Morning" to me, and I had responded with the bird . . . twice. All I could do was offer some sort of laugh to try to hide my sheer embarrassment. I couldn't believe that happened. I put my hands up in the air, palms facing him, begging for his forgiveness. He laughed back equally as heartily and we gave each other a high five. Our friendship had just transitioned to its next phase.

As I shared the story, the room erupted into laughter. People were wiping the joy tears from their eyes. It was a big hit.

I turned and gave David a big hug and we shared a special moment. Then I walked back to my booth and sat next to Patty to whisper, "Babe, I am going to kill you."

Many of us go through our day isolated from the world by our own little private bubbles. We have our routines;

we drive the same routes to work or to school or to the store; we order the same meals at the same restaurants; we watch the same shows. We are locked into our own little worlds—horse blinders and all.

At the same time, life seems to be getting faster and faster, and we're getting busier and busier, so we live with a constant sense that we never have enough time. To counter this feeling, we want everything quicker. We microwave, we drive-through, we look for the shortest line, we drive over the speed limit.

Add to the mix the beautiful 4K-and-up screens of our smartphones that are always in our hands, and all of this has left us disconnected and unaware of the amazing beauty and life that surrounds us every single day. The fact is that unless you never leave your home, you come in contact with so many people every day, yet there is a good chance that you don't even notice. Tragically, though, in not noticing, we miss out on so many wonders and moments in life. We also miss out on countless opportunities to be of service and to let helping people know how much they matter.

The thought of never knowing David completely bums me out. I know that David knows how much he matters to me, and I know how much I matter to him. And the thought of not looking up and seeing Bear crossing the street with enough time to stop my car is . . . well, I just won't go there.

So start looking up. Give someone a compliment. Wish someone a "Nice day!" And please stop staring down your baristas with the hopes that you will get your coffee quicker. You won't. Instead, try saying, "Hello" to them and even consider asking them a question. You never know, it just might be the only "Hello" or question they get from a customer all day.

When we look up, we can see. When we see, we can sense. When we sense, we can be of service.

TAKE ACTION

Think of someone that you see every day but you haven't taken the time to truly get to know yet. Maybe it is someone at the dry cleaners, the security guard at work, the teller at your bank, your gardener, or your mail-delivery person. In doing this, you will probably be shocked at how many people you encounter on any given day, and how many of them work in service positions and serve you. Think of a way to make sure they know how much they matter to you the next time you see them. It will be an incredible and meaningful surprise for them. Be creative. Be caring. Be cool.

JOURNAL ENTRY

Write about a time when someone looked up and noticed you. No, not in a bar or at a restaurant and they were picking up on you. I mean a time when someone really noticed you and took the time to make sure you knew how much you mattered. Maybe it was the first day at a new job or school or new church. Heck, maybe it was your new local Starbucks. What did they do to make you feel noticed? Was it a simple gesture or something more than that? How did it make you feel? How has it, if at all, helped you connect with how you can do the same thing for others? P.S.: If it hasn't, let this be a kind kick in the butt to start doing it now.

CONVERSATION STARTER

On a scale of 1–10, with 10 being "high," how would you score yourself when it comes to being aware of and connecting with your surroundings? What can you do to be better at looking around and engaging?

8

Be There

BE A FRIEND
TO HAVE A FRIEND

I would rather walk with a friend in the
dark than walk alone in the light.

—Helen Keller

Life is not meant to be done alone. We are social creatures
and need one another deeply in order to survive and hopefully thrive. Sorry, introverts, this applies to you as well. The
problem is that we keep doing everything possible to keep
ourselves from being in community, from having friends.
Instead, we simply complain, "It's really hard to make
friends nowadays." I hear this all the time, and it drives
me nuts. I have a solution: Stop complaining about not

having friends, and instead flip the script and say, "Today, I am going to focus on being someone's friend." No more victim mentality. No more sitting at home and waiting for a new friend to knock on the door. Not only will this decrease the complaining, it will increase the friending.

My father shared this concept with my brother and me at an early age. I will never forget his nugget of advice: "You have to be a friend to have a friend." Seriously one of the best lessons I've ever learned. Somehow I have also combined this statement with the infamous quote, "Be the change you wish to see in the world." I say, "Be the friend you wish to have in the world."

But being a friend is not always easy. We have all been hurt by friends before. They have broken our trust. They haven't shown up when we needed them most. Feel familiar? But we can't let these scars keep us from engaging with one another. We still have to offer our fullest selves, vulnerabilities, fears, and all in order to create the friendships we all so desperately want and need.

We also can't keep fooling ourselves that friendships on social media are actually the deep and life-giving friendships that we need. Sorry, no one can have a thousand-plus true friends; friendship isn't about quantity, it's about quality. If anything, time spent on social media "friends" only takes away from the little extra time we have to actually build real friendships, thereby leaving us connected, yet so disconnected.

At the risk of sounding like an old fuddy-duddy, I

remember a time when most of us knew our neighbors. We knew their names. We borrowed things from them, like milk or flour. We even got their mail for them when they went out of town. Oh, the brilliance of Mr. Rogers—"Won't you be my neighbor?" Not today. A recent study from Pew Research Center shows that only 31 percent of Americans say they know all or most of their neighbors—40 percent in rural areas, 24 percent in urban neighborhoods. That is the craziest thought to me. And as our urban populations continue to grow, the percentage of those who know their neighbors will continue to drop.

Why is this happening? Is it because we don't trust one another anymore? Again, we've been hurt . . . even by friendships. We have gone from "knock on my door anytime" to "knock on my door only when it is light out" to "never knock on my door." Or is it because of the invention of the electric garage door in 1926 by C. G. Johnson that allows us to go to and from our home without having to ever see a soul?

I think it could be a little bit of all of these reasons; however, these are just excuses. The real reason this has happened is because we have not taken the time to proactively step outside and introduce ourselves to our neighbors. We have not placed a "So happy to be your neighbor" card on their front door. We have not organized a block party. This is why we don't know our neighbors. We haven't tried to. This is also why we don't feel like we have enough real friends. We have to own it in order for it and us to change . . . even when it's not asked of us.

*   *   *

I never get the best of feelings driving to cemeteries, but
it is one of those things we get to do in life. I say "get" to
because it really is a beautiful gesture and opportunity
to honor those we have lost and their survivors. Plus, it
is arguably one of the most profound ways to let people
know they matter to you. In this case, I was going to
Forest Lawn to honor my friend Rob Lo, who had lost
his father.

There are a few details about this particular funeral
that are important to know. First of all, I never met Rob's
father. Second, I really didn't know Rob all that well.
He was part of the WeHo Swimming Pool Mötley Crüe.
Again, we all knew one another, but it was always more
like, "Hey, how are you? How's your week going? Feel
like going hard or taking it easy in the pool today? Nice
work. Great workout. Have a good night." Obviously, the
act of swimming doesn't allow much conversation, either,
so that doesn't help. But Rob had mentioned to us that
his father passed away and said he posted details on his
Facebook page. Which leads me to the third factor—that
Rob did not know I was going to be there. I figured I
would just surprise him, and hopefully that would cheer
him up.

So there I was, inside the pearly gates of Forest Lawn
looking for the Lo family burial, knowing that the only
person I would probably know would be Rob himself. I
saw a large gathering of Chinese people off in the distance,

so I drove in that direction and parked my car. It appeared as though they were just getting started, so I slowly walked up to the back of the group to quietly assimilate into the standing audience. There were easily over one hundred people standing and facing the casket, with the family sitting in chairs in front of us, also facing the casket. It was kind of a relief they had their backs to us, because I didn't want Rob to know I was a minute or two late.

A few things became instantly obvious to me. First, the funeral officiate was not speaking English, so I was not going to understand much. Second, I was the only Caucasian person there and the only person six feet three inches tall and not wearing a black suit with a black tie. So much for my assimilation plan. But after acknowledging a few folks with a simple nod of my head and subtle smile, I felt right at home.

The service was beautiful. I joined the chorus of voices as we sang "Amazing Grace" (with me singing in English). I cried just because so many people around me were crying. I felt the love that this man spread in the world, and I grieved for my friend Rob. Clearly this was a tough day for everyone, and as each minute went by, I was so happy I decided to be there.

After the speaking parts were over, three Forest Lawn employees quietly worked their way through the standing audience to give each of us a red rose. The officiate then clearly explained, in Chinese, that first the family would say their final goodbyes by approaching the beautiful black casket and placing their roses on top, and then the rest of us would follow. I anxiously waited as the family stood up, backs facing us, and walked around to the other side of the casket to face us and say their goodbyes.

Wait, where was Rob? How was it possible that he wasn't at his father's funeral? This was terrible. I pulled one of the Forest Lawn employees aside and asked, "Is this the funeral for Mr. Lo?" She replied, "No. This is burial for Mr. Woo. The Lo burial starts in ten minutes over there," pointing to a hill directly behind us.

I turned around to see where she was pointing, and sure enough another gathering of black-haired, black-suit-and-tie-wearing, and shorter-than-me people were starting to gather. I had just attended the burial of a complete stranger. No wonder I received those interesting looks upon my initial approach. I was a funeral crasher. But I cried. I sang. I felt so much sadness for this family. Well, I thought it was for Rob, but no, it was for a family of strangers. "Now what do I do?"

I slowly and calmly took a few steps backward, nonchalantly looking down at the tombstones that surrounded us, to seem somewhat somber and reflective, but also not to make eye contact with anyone else. Then, when I was finally at the very back of the pack, I noticed a tombstone without any flowers on it. I gently placed my red rose on it, and started a beeline directly to the Lo burial and never looked back.

As I approached the Lo burial I immediately spotted

Rob and he spotted me. He started walking toward me with a big smile on his face. I was still a good thirty yards out. He gave me a big hug and thanked me for being there. He was truly surprised, and clearly my being there moved him. And then he said, "But why are you walking from over there?"

I looked at him and said, "Rob, you have no idea what just happened."

When I say that my breakdown has changed me for the better, what I really mean is that it has changed how I interact with people. For starters, my empathy and compassion for others is stronger than ever. Now, whenever I see someone, even a total stranger, I do all I can to make sure they feel seen in that moment. It's almost as if I am saying to them, "I am here and willing to be your friend." It might be a simple smile and a hello. Yes, even in an elevator. I am that person who talks in elevators, and it freaks Patty out. I can hear her now: "Babe, you're not supposed to talk to people in an elevator. It's creepy." What? That is the dumbest thing I have ever heard. What's creepy to me is the idea that I am supposed to stand in this moving five-by-eight-foot box, stare at the numbers above the door like I am hypnotized, and pretend like the person standing three feet from me doesn't even exist. Now that is strange.

I have also been known to grab people by their wenus. Calm down . . . a wenus is that random fold of skin on your elbow. For some reason, pinching someone's wenus always makes them smile. Just try it sometime. And I'm not afraid to slap a buddy on the ass and say, "Good game," even though we didn't play a game or sport of any kind. I do these things because they create laughter. They catch people off guard and get them out of their heads (or bubbles) to just be present and feel joy for a second. Of course, I also do the more meaningful things like ask questions, call people on the phone—even when it's not on their calendar—and tell people that I love them.

The good news is that I certainly don't have a patent on these techniques. So try them out and have fun with it. I promise you that your current friendships will flourish and new ones will start to grow. Be the friend first; people are just waiting for the invitation . . . to know that they matter to you.

The Lo burial was equally as beautiful as the Woo burial. Once again, I didn't understand a word. I stood out like a sore thumb. I cried. And this time I actually got to put my new red rose on the casket it was intended for.

After the ceremony concluded, Rob grabbed me and said he wanted to introduce me to his family. Well, he introduced me for sure, but he also told them all about my Woo experience. The family completely lost it. I'm not sure that the Forest Lawn grounds have ever heard such a roar of laughter. All I could do was join in the chorus of laughter, even though it was clearly at my expense . . . a situation I often find myself in and something I clearly got from my mother. Love you, Mom.

Then Rob said to me, "Thank you for bringing me joy on this day. A day I did not think joy was even possible." Then he offered: "My family thanks you too and has invited you to our private family lunch. They would be honored to have you." Of course I accepted the offer. I was honored to be a part of the Lo family.

Yes, sometimes you have to be a friend to have a friend . . . even if it means attending the wrong funeral.

TAKE ACTION

Think of a friend that you have not been in touch with in over a year. Call that person to check in. Convey that you were thinking about him or her and wanted to catch up. Better yet, if the person lives near you, go out to lunch or for coffee and spend some quality time together. And when you see or talk to the person, ask him or her what you can do to be an even better friend. Have you ever been asked that question by a friend before? It's gonna be good. Oh, and for the record, if the friend is within an hour's drive, that's still "near" you, so make it a face-to-face experience.

JOURNAL ENTRY

What keeps you from being more outgoing when it comes to being or making friends? Get honest with yourself here. Is it something from your past? Maybe a past hurt or disappointment from a friend? Write yourself a permission slip to officially let go of that past hurt, disappointment, fear, experience, etc. If you're not sure you should write it, don't worry; I am giving you full permission to move on and thrive again. We all need meaningful friendships in our life. We can't let anything get in the way.

CONVERSATION STARTER

Do you think social media has been helpful or harmful for growing meaningful relationships? Why or why not?

Be Present

MOMENTS MATTER

I'm not trying to be efficient; I'm trying to
be present.

—Bob Goff

This past New Year's, Patty and I made what might have
been the best resolution either of us has ever made. Like
most people, we have typically gone for the lose-some-
weight, stop-a-bad-habit, or make-more-money options.
After all, who doesn't want to be healthier and wealthier?
But this year we did something different. We resolved to
start a new hobby. When was the last time you had a hobby
and really dove into it? No, not like the once-every-few-
months sort of commitment, but a genuine and honest effort? For me, the answer was easy: a really really long time.

Patty decided she wanted to learn how to play the banjo. For the record, this might have been one of the coolest things she has ever said. Don't get me wrong, my wife is supercool and sexy, but banjo? Really? This is right up there with the time we were visiting a pumpkin patch for Halloween and she came walking around the corner holding a full-grown goat in her arms. I was sold.

Just to provide a little context, Patty's family is from a small area on the border of Georgia and North Carolina called "Lickin' Log Gap." I don't know much about Lickin' Log Gap. I'm not even sure there is much to know about it. But what I do know is that her family loved sittin' on the front porch and havin' a cookout, all the while pluckin' on their banjos and singin'. Bluegrass music was alive and well in Lickin' Log Gap, so Patty has it in her soul.

My hobby might not be as cool and sexy, but it has been beyond life-giving for me. When my brother and I were little, my mom and dad used to take us to golf and tennis camp during the summers. I never really took to golf, probably because I was too hyper for it, but I always loved the tennis part of camp. I remember my parents buying me my first and only tennis racquet, a Donnay Borg Pro. Not to date myself, but Bjorn Borg's tennis career was at its peak in the late seventies, so this goes back a few years. But my Donnay Borg Pro was beautiful. Wood covered by black graphite with red and orange stripes along the head of the racquet. I don't know why or how, but I still have that racquet today, and it is still supercool to me. So logically, of course—or maybe not at all—I decided it was time for me to pick up tennis again. After all, it has only been a short forty-year break.

Although our new hobbies couldn't be more different, they have been the biggest blessings and have connected us in new ways. Patty has been able to express her creative side more and reconnect with her family roots. I've been able to get great exercise and make new friends, something I felt missing in my life. The Toluca Lake Tennis & Fitness Club became my new West Hollywood Pool. Perfect.

Every Saturday and Sunday morning, we meet at the club in the morning to play. It is an awesome group of people, from starving artists to uber-successful businessmen and women, young and old, tall and short, white, brown, and black, gay and straight, good and great tennis players. We truly cover the entire spectrum. But we come together every weekend to play "drop-ins." This means we just show up, see who is there, and then we put games together and have at it. It's just like pickup basketball.

On this particular Saturday, I was paired up with a gentleman named Mehran. Mehran is a sixty-year-old gentleman from Iran. He's built like a tank or a middle linebacker—broad shoulders, thick, strong. But he also has slicked-back longish gray hair, gray scruff for a beard, and wears really small round-lensed glasses with silver frames, so he also has this Santa Claus–like warmth and approachability. I didn't know Mehran very well, but we always acknowledged one another with a welcoming gesture and chatted from time to time. But this day was going to be the day we got to connect a little more. After all, we were doubles partners.

After a good ninety minutes of playing tennis, Mehran and I sat down to relax with a cold glass of water and our typical club-issued white towels. For a moment we relived the highlights on the court, then Mehran said, "Hey, Matt, I have a question for you." I replied, "Great, hopefully I have an answer." Mehran continued, "I know we don't know one another very well, but I believe you are the right person to ask." At this stage of our friendship, Mehran had no idea what I did for a living, so believing I was the right person was peculiar to me, but I went with it. Then he asked the question: "Matt, do you think life gets easier or harder as you get older?"

I took a sip of water, wiped my face with my towel, and said, "You know, Mehran, that is a pretty big question, so I would probably need a moment to think about it and get back to you." But then I realized that I had to give him something. I felt that the only reason someone would ask this question is because his or her life seemed to be getting harder, not easier. And as I looked into his eyes through his tiny glasses, I saw a man who needed answers. He needed my attention—undistracted, fully committed, fully focused, fully present.

I often travel up to Northern California for business meetings or to see my family. We live right by Bob Hope

Airport, which is our favorite airport in the country. It's as if Bob Hope built it himself fifty years ago and it hasn't changed or grown since. So if I can grab a flight out of Bob Hope instead of Los Angeles International Airport (LAX), I jump at the opportunity.

Besides its ease of use, the other spectacular part of Bob Hope Airport is that you board (and exit) your plane on the tarmac. Yep, they still wheel those mobile staircases up to the plane and you walk across the blacktop until you reach that first stair to head up to the plane. And if that's not cool enough as is, Bob Hope Airport also boards from both the front and the rear of the plane. So cool.

Since I am six feet three and weigh a solid 230 pounds, I always book the aisle seat when I fly. Water polo also did a nice job of broadening my shoulders, so it's nice to have that extra width as well. So, per usual, I found myself sitting in my aisle seat as the rest of the passengers filed onboard.

On a recent trip, we sat on the tarmac for longer than usual, which can often mean some sort of problem with the plane or a late passenger. Again, it's Bob Hope Airport, so they are cool like that with people running a little late. But sitting on the tarmac is never good for the mood onboard. The plane heats up because the doors are open and the AC is off. People get restless and start wondering what's causing the delay. Some people even decide to use the restroom, which gets the flight attendants a little miffed because they are trying to get everyone in their seats. Quite the perfect storm for grumpiness on board.

Then we found the culprit. In a huff, a final frantic passenger ran onto the plane. He was a younger guy, maybe thirty years old or so, dressed all in black with long stringy black hair and a chin beard that went down to the middle of his belly. As I watched him make his way down the aisle, I could see the stress on his face, and when he took the aisle seat across from mine, I began to feel it.

He jammed one of his bags in the overhead bin above me and the gentleman in front of me, then he stuffed his other bag under the chair in front of him. Everything about his movements was unstable and unsettled. He slammed his phone on the arm of his chair a bunch of times. He stomped his foot on the ground as if he were playing the drums. He rocked forward and backward, tapping his forehead on the back of the seat in front of him. And he couldn't stop pulling on his chin beard.

As I watched longer, I began to notice that people around us were starting to get upset. They started tossing out short remarks, giving him dirty looks, and seemingly pondering if there was an empty seat somewhere else on the plane to move to. And all of this was taking place before we even started to roll back from the gate.

As I sat there, I kept going back and forth between *I know what it is like to feel uncomfortable or anxious on an airplane, so I feel bad for him and wonder if I can help* and *This guy is going to cause a fight, and I am going to involuntarily end up in someone's cell phone video of a fight breaking out on a plane while up in the air.* Surely nothing good was going to happen next.

Then he pulled out the airline magazine in the fold in

front of him and started ripping the pages out. One by one, he yanked at the pages, swearing with every new page, absolutely causing a commotion. He was literally having a fight with a magazine, and people were freaked out. But then, just as I thought all hell was going to break loose, something magical happened. As he yanked another page of the magazine out, he came to the crossword-puzzle page and stopped. Yes, every airline magazine has a crossword-puzzle page, and now I have a new appreciation for it.

He looked at the puzzle for a minute and then started rummaging through his belongings to look for a pen or pencil. The longer he looked the more aggressive he got. Oh, no, he didn't have a pen or pencil. Now what to do? I immediately engaged, grabbed a pen from my bag, and said, "Hey, man, it seems like you were looking for a pen to do that crossword puzzle. Here, use mine."

For the first time we made eye contact, which was subtly scary for me, and he said, "Thanks, man, I really appreciate that" and took my pen.

Just when I thought I had saved the day, he looked back at me less than a minute later and said, "Hey, here is your pen back. I don't think I have the energy to do that puzzle right now, but I really appreciate it," and he handed me my pen.

At this point, I had a decision to make. Either I take the pen and just ignore him, or I keep engaging him. I decided on the latter. "So, are you traveling up north for business or do you live up there and are just flying home?"

Rich and I never stopped talking for the entire flight. He completely relaxed. His feet stopped stomping the ground, his hands rested peacefully on his legs, he smiled, laughed, and truly connected. I found out he is a business owner and married with two young children. And, even nicer, he asked questions about my life and me. He was a true gentleman with a great soul.

I also learned something else about Rich that helped make sense to his actions: he suffers from Asperger syndrome. Both of his children suffer from it as well. We never talked about his dramatic entrance onto the plane, but it was understood that certain things, like flying, are not easy for him and he was experiencing a real moment.

Right before deplaning, Rich gave me his business card and said, "It was so nice meeting you," almost in acknowledgement that it was a moment that mattered to him.

As Mehran and I drank our water, I attempted to answer his question. "I believe that life does get more complicated as we get older. With every year of life, we have new experiences, new joys, new sorrows, new bumps and bruises, new questions. It's just part of being human. What I believe determines whether these experiences make life easier or harder is our perspective. Because if our perspective doesn't change, if we don't start to redefine things, like what it means to be successful and to live a good life, then life can get really hard."

Mehran's eyes started to tear up, and I could feel his heaviness. Our conversation continued, and I learned that he is a successful architect who specializes in skyscrapers.

Randomly enough, I know a bit about the narcissistic and ego-driven essence of the skyscraper world, and talking about it with Mehran certainly brought us a good chuckle. I also learned that Mehran and his wife were about to be empty nesters—typically not the easiest adjustment to make.

I shared with Mehran some ideas about how we spend our entire life trying to achieve, trying to reach some level of "success," and we never seem to find it. We are never "enough." We never have "enough." And we are left feeling empty and confused, because life doesn't seem to get better, only harder. I encouraged Mehran to discover how to bring more purpose and significance into his life, and I shared a little bit about my story with the hopes that it would help.

Mehran thanked me for my time and my honest answer and stood up to give me the biggest bear hug. The conversation meant a lot to him . . . and to me. It was a moment that mattered to both of us.

Life is defined by moments. Especially ones that matter. One of the greatest gifts we can give to one another is our undivided attention. First of all, this means we are giving of our time—time that we will never get back. Second, it communicates that whatever others' needs are in the given moment, we are there for them, and they matter. But how often do we get that present with people? How often do we completely shut everything else out, from our devices to our thoughts to our needs, to just be in the moment—to be truly connected and be there for someone? The truth is—not enough.

It's time for us to be more present. To connect more deeply with one another and to create meaningful moments that can lead to meaningful relationships. For without these, life can be a real bitch . . . at any point in the journey.

TAKE ACTION

Establish a "Be-Present Buddy" system with someone in your life. The goal is to create a buddy system with someone wherein both parties agree to truly be present with one another in special circumstances. Of course, we all want to be this way with all of our interactions and relationships at all times, but this is different. This is the person that you can go to when you are having a tough moment, making a big life decision, or simply feeling the need for some focused connection. This system is an agreement to be that rock for one another—to listen without judgment or distraction and to provide loving feedback and opinions. This is about moments that matter.

JOURNAL ENTRY

Write down and answer each of these questions:

When was a time when you really needed someone to be present for you and they weren't? What happened, and how did it make you feel?

When was a time when you really needed someone to be present for you and they were? What happened, and how did it make you feel?

When was a time when someone needed you to be present for them and you weren't? What happened, and how did it make you feel?

When was a time when someone needed you to be present for them and you were? What happened, and how did it make you feel?

CONVERSATION STARTER

What are some pet peeves you have around trying to have an in-person conversation with someone? For example, when people constantly interrupt, when people continually look at their phone or over your shoulder? When people don't take their sunglasses off? Sorry, those are just a few of my peeves. See how many you can come up with. Then, oh boy, see how many of them you do yourself. Have fun with it, but learn and grow from it, too.

10

Be Creative
WRITE IT OUT

No act of kindness, no matter how
small . . . is ever wasted.

—AESOP

It was an exciting time in Modesto, California, for the
Emerzian family. My Grandma Flo was turning ninety
years young, and we were ready to celebrate.

I loved both my grandmothers. Anahid, aka "Grandma
Annie" or "Annie Bananie," was my mom's mom. A total
kick in the pants. A prankster who laughed so hard at her
own jokes and pranks that she often peed her pants. All she
needed was herself and an unexpected victim. Florence, aka
"Grandma Flo" or "Flo Mo," on the other hand, always
had everything in order. Flo had her own dry wit, but it

was her brainpower that always caught our attention. Sharp as a tack. Memory like a steal trap. The City of Modesto bridge champion several times over.

Flo also loved her birthdays, especially when people remembered and sent her birthday cards. She could never get enough birthday cards and tallied the stack of cards each and every year. Since turning ninety was a biggie, my mom came up with a great idea and reached out to most of the people she *and* Flo knew and asked them to send Flo a birthday card. Drumroll, please . . .

On her ninetieth birthday, Grandma Flo received a record-breaking 107 birthday cards. She could not have been happier.

I remember her saying, "I can't believe all of these people remembered my birthday," with a huge smile on her face and a subtle surprised look on her face. She felt as though she was on top of the world. My mom pulled off arguably one of the best birthday gifts I have ever heard of. Brilliant.

Robert and I had lunch together at least once a week at his favorite spot, Stanley's on Ventura Boulevard. When we walked in the door, it was as if royalty had arrived. It was, after all, Robert Kardashian. But Robert never saw it that way and never treated anyone as though he was above them. Rather, Robert said hello to everyone and treated everyone like family. He knew the hostesses, the servers, the chefs, and the owners; and each of them had the opportunity to experience his huge smile and caring eyes. And with everything and anything they said to him, he always replied, "That's good!" or "That's a good thing!" In other words, he lit up the room and lifted everyone's spirits within seconds.

As Robert and I sat and enjoyed our chopped salads, Robert's favorite Stanley's meal, I noticed he was struggling slightly with his swallowing. I watched him strain. I watched him try to clear his throat. And occasionally I would see him wince. Realizing I was almost finished with my salad and that he still had more than half of his on his plate, I decided to ask him if he was okay.

Robert shared, "When we were in Lake Como, I started having a tough time swallowing certain foods, like bread." Robert had just returned from a two-week vacation in Italy—a trip he had been looking forward to for years. I asked him if he had seen the doctor, and he said he hadn't yet but planned on it. He got a to-go container for the rest of his salad, and we headed to the office to get back to work.

A week later, Robert came into my office to say something I still wish I'd never heard. He said, "Hey, buddy, so remember my swallowing thing? Well, it turns out that I have esophageal cancer and today is my first chemo treatment."

Shocked and choked up, I looked him in the eye and said, "You be strong and trust that you will get through this." To which he replied, "If the cancer and chemo don't kill me, the thought of you running my company certainly does, so I plan on healing." He left my office with that same huge grin, and he left me believing, just like everyone else he touched, that everything would be good.

Sadly, those were the last words Robert ever said to me. And it was the last time I would see him until the day before he passed away, just five weeks later.

Robert had an aggressive cancer that attacked his system so feverishly that he literally lost fifty pounds in five weeks and didn't want any of us to see him that way. Every day when we walked into the office, we would get updates from his daughters, or Barb, his longtime assistant. And each time we were delivered another blow. It wasn't going well.

But I had to do something. I loved this man. He was a friend. A mentor. One of the kindest and most caring people I had ever met. He loved his family and he loved life, and he gave me a big break in my career, for which I will be forever grateful. Sitting on the sidelines wasn't going to work for me.

One day, while driving home from work, inspired by my mom's birthday-card secret for Grandma Flo, I decided to add my own little twist to it. See, my Grandpa Charlie, Annie's husband, died of leukemia. The doctors told him he had six months to live, but he lived for over thirteen years. And I don't mean that he was alive for thirteen more years; rather, that he truly lived them. He still went to work every day and helped his son Matty, my uncle, run the family business. Rain or shine, he attended the games and special events for his grandchildren, Chad and Brady. And he still drove around Fresno and delivered boxes of apples to friends and families. His love for life and for people, coupled with toughness and a positive attitude, allowed my grandfather to shatter his six-month life sentence. I believed Robert could do the same.

So my friend Kelly and I came up with the idea to create and print five-by-seven-inch inspirational cards that I could mail to Robert every day on my way to work. The cards included inspirational quotes, song lyrics, Bible verses, and more. Anything to lift his spirits. And every morning on my way to work, I dropped one card in a blue roadside mailbox. I did it this way because I didn't put a return address on the envelopes, and I didn't want him to see a West Hollywood Post Office stamp on the envelopes, either. Robert was sharp and he would have known they were from me otherwise.

Every morning, for four and a half weeks, I pulled my car over and dropped a card in the little blue slot. I never missed a day. At the office, I would occasionally hear someone talking about these "supercool cards that my dad was receiving," but no one knew who was sending them. I just kept about my work and never said a word, hoping the cards were working. But then I received a call from Robert's family to let me know that he was most likely in his final hours and that they wanted me to come to the house to say my goodbyes.

As the family escorted me into Robert's room to say goodbye, the first thing I saw was Robert himself, lying in a hospital bed they'd brought in for him. Of course, my heart sank. There was no doubt that he was ready to pass.

But then my eyes peeled away from his face and slowly panned up the wall next to his bed, and what I saw took my breath away. There they were . . . my cards. Over four weeks of them, taped to the wall right beside him so he could read each and every one of them.

With tears streaming down my face, I looked back down at his face. His eyes opened, and I gave him a little wry smile, as if to say, "Yep, maybe I am the person who sent you those." I then told him how much I loved him, kissed him on his forehead, and left.

A week later I stood in the cemetery for Robert's funeral service with a stack of seven unsent cards in my hand. I felt they belonged to Robert, so I decided to place them on top of his casket. But then, in the last moment, I decided to keep one of them to hand to his family.

This particular card was one of my favorites, and I wanted them to have it. It was a line from a famous song about being in times of trouble and in darkness, and having Mary come to comfort and speak wise words. I think you know the song. You see, The Beatles were Robert's favorite band, and "Let It Be" was his favorite song.

As we finished our final goodbyes and enjoyed one final moment with Robert together, the speakers turned on and, as a group, we stood silently and listened to "Let It Be" by The Beatles—the only song we heard the entire service.

Grandma Flo lived three more years, following her nine-tieth birthday. Even until the very end, she never lost her

sharpness. I will never forget walking into her hospital room
to be greeted by Flo and a lineup of nurses that she wanted
me to meet. For over fifteen years, she told me that she was
not going to leave this world until she knew I met a special
girl to marry. I quickly learned that these poor nurses had
to hear my life story several times over, look at pictures of
me that she'd brought with her, and embarrassingly gather
in her hospital room in preparation for my arrival.

Although Flo never made it as a successful marriage-
partner fixer-upper in her final days, she did do something
that continues to bless all of us profoundly. After her passing, and upon going through her home, we discovered a
little hidden gem that she left behind. My grandmother
saved every single card she had ever gotten, including the
107 cards she'd received on her ninetieth birthday. Better
yet, she had all of the cards organized in old shoeboxes,
sorted by the name of the sender. Meaning each family
member was gifted back every card or note they had ever
sent Flo.

I know these cards meant a lot to her when she received
them, but I could argue that receiving them back from
her was even more meaningful. I now get to sit with my
rubber-banded stack of cards to reread and relive so many
special moments with my grandmother. I can so vividly see
where I was sitting when I wrote each card. The words remind me of the deep love I felt for her, and the sheer number of thank-you notes is simply a symbol of her generosity.
I am so grateful for Flo and her cards. And much like Flo
never knew my mom "recruited" so many people to send

her a ninetieth birthday card, we never knew Flo had filled shoeboxes waiting for us.

There is something special about handwritten notes. They can't be written with our thumbs. They can't be deleted by the press of a button. And, truth be told, they are unfortunately rare, borderline extinct, these days. But we are powerful with a piece of paper and a pen in our hand. It gives us great agency to lovingly and kindly let someone else know how much they matter to us. Even a tiny note written with a Sharpie on a Post-it Note can brighten someone's day.

So put down your phone. Stop typing on your keyboard. Reconnect with the joy you felt when you first learned how to write cursive in the third grade. Think about someone in your life, or several people, who would love nothing more than to receive a handwritten note from you. Then, of course, take a meaningful moment to write and deliver your little gift.

Just be prepared for how special it is going to be for both you and the person you wrote it to.

TAKE ACTION

Write out a list of five people in your life, alive or passed on, from whom it would mean the world to you to receive a handwritten, heartfelt note. Got your list? Perfect. Now go write and deliver one to each of them. I promise it will mean the world to them as well.

Write yourself a letter and include some of the following ideas, or anything else that comes to mind:

- Who are you right in this moment? How do you spend your time?
- What are you goals for the next year? Dreams?
- What makes you happy? What challenges you?
- How would you like to grow?

Once you have written the letter, sign it "You Matter," with your name and the date. Then put it in an envelope and mail it to yourself. Here is the final important challenge: Don't open it until exactly one year from today.

When is the last time you received a handwritten note or card from someone? Who was it from, and how did it make you feel?

PART THREE

We Matter

We are part of something bigger.

We are *we* because of one another.

We are stronger together.

We have much to learn.

We have more to give.

We matter.

Be Brave
SHOW UP ANYWAY

The ultimate measure of a man is not where he stands in moments of convenience and comfort, but where he stands at times of challenge and controversy.

—Martin Luther King, Jr.
(etched in stone on the north wall of the MLK, Jr. Memorial in Washington, DC)

It's so hard to explain the brutal grips of an anxiety attack to someone who has never experienced one. The sweaty hands, tight chest, and labored breathing are the easy parts to explain and endure, for that matter. After all, they are just physical symptoms that most people can relate to. It's the suffering that takes place between the ears that is so crippling and challenging to put into words.

I met a twenty-year-old marine who had recently returned from a tour of duty in the Middle East. His armored vehicle had hit an IED, and he lost the lower half of one of his legs and both of his arms. We sat and talked for a while, and he clearly got it. He said, "War is brutal, and most of us come home with wounds. I am just glad my wounds are on the outside."

Anxiety shrank my world. Every day my safe place got smaller and smaller, and as the walls of my world closed in, I found my bedroom was the only place I felt safe. This doesn't bode well for living a normal life. But over time, as I healed, the walls started to expand again. I could leave my room and even my house. I could drive again and even grin and bear traffic. I could get in an elevator and take the Metro. And eventually I was able to conquer my final frontier—flying. I knew that the day I would be able to comfortably get on a plane again would also be the day I was healthy again.

I started small, with short, one-hour flights. Then two-hour, and eventually cross-country ones. I can't say that I ever loved it, but I was able to let go of control just enough to white-knuckle my way through it. A little courage and a half of Xanax seemed to be the winning combination. But just when I thought I was through the weeds and all was back to normal, I had another panic attack while boarding a flight from Los Angeles to Montgomery, Alabama, and my world shrank again. I guess I wasn't ready, and it hurt me deeply. I was still broken and needed more work.

For four years from that day I refused to fly. This was a disaster for someone who makes a living doing keynotes and also runs an organization that serves people nationwide. I was literally leaving money on the table and limiting my impact on people's lives because of my fear. Even worse, I felt like a failure, and I wondered if my life would ever be normal again. Would I have to change my career? Would I ever be able to fulfill my promise of taking Patty to Europe for her first time? So many questions and not a single answer that I liked.

But deep down, I knew that the only solution was to face and conquer my fear. So, with the support of my wife, my family, and a few friends who knew my secret, I set out to do just that. I did hypnosis, past-life regression, mantra meditation, crystal work, spiritual work, praying, tapping. You name it, I tried it. And then the day of truth came. I needed to be in Dallas to do a keynote for an influential national women's group. I was all in. Contract signed. Name and bio printed in the program. Check received. There was no turning back.

Getting to the airport that morning was fairly smooth. I felt ready. I had put in the work. However, with every step closer to my seat on the plane, I could feel the pressure start to mount. From parking to security to the line at Starbucks to first boarding call, my breathing got shorter, my vision blurrier, my thoughts more scattered. I started to break.

As they made the final boarding call, it became clear to me that I, 1,000 percent, could not step foot on the plane. I was a complete mess—crying, pacing the terminal floor, dry-heaving. Patty, bless her heart, was trying to do and say all the right things. She called my parents and had me talk to them. She consoled me and tried to help me trust that it would be okay. She even tried to buy some extra time with the gate agents—anything to gently and lovingly give me the time and opportunity to get on that plane. Again, it's next to impossible to explain the panic and the war raging in your mind when full-blown panic has set in. So it's also hard for people to know how to help. But Patty was being my rock. And then two things happened that changed everything.

I started texting with our dear friend Sophie and shared my struggles. She was one of the friends who knew this was a big day for me. Sophie texted, "Matt, this is not about you or the flight. This is about you being of service. There are lives in Dallas that are waiting for and needing to hear your message. Go serve them. It is your calling." And then she wrote, "Take it one step at a time. What can you do right now to get yourself on that plane? What is one thing you can do?"

Then Patty came up with the most brilliant answer ever: "I am going to ask the gate agents if they will allow you to walk onto the plane and sit in your seat to see how it feels. If you don't like it, we can leave. How is that for a next step?"

I loved the idea and immediately uncurled myself from

my mess of a ball, grabbed my stuff, and walked toward the gate. We walked down the tunnel, boarded the plane, sat in our seats, and took inventory together.

As I looked around the plane, saw Patty's comforting and caring gaze, and thought of Sophie's words about the lives waiting to be touched, I looked at Patty and said, "I'm good. Let's do this." And in that moment my anxiety vanished. As hard as it had hit, it disappeared equally as fast. Three hours later we landed in Dallas, Texas. Today, five years later, I haven't stop flying.

I know that politics and religion are two topics most people recommend not discussing. And this book is certainly not a religious or political book. However, I was with my family in Washington, DC, on Election Day 2016.

The day after the election, I remember being in a café, and the gentleman in front of me in line asked the barista if they sold something stronger than coffee. I remember standing outside the White House while my mom and Patty hugged a pregnant woman who was sobbing and uttering the words, "How will I ever explain this to my daughter?" as she rubbed her stomach. I remember being inside the National Museum of African American History and Culture that afternoon and watching Patty being consoled by an elderly African American woman who told her, "Don't worry, baby, we have survived far worse. We will all get through this together." Finally, I remember standing in front of the Martin Luther King, Jr. Memorial on this same gray, dreary day, as the rainwater gathered under the lower lid of his right eye and eventually started streaming down his cheek as if he were crying.

I have spent the last ten years of my life inspiring people to embrace how much and why they matter. I have helped people who didn't feel like they mattered know that they do. I've also tried to help people who thought they mattered for all the wrong reasons—like greed, ego, money, and power—try to discover why they really matter.

By the end of the day, we were all exhausted physically and emotionally, and we called it a day. Plus, I had to leave early the next morning because I was delivering an inspirational keynote to a large community bank about four hours outside of DC. Patty and I said goodbye to my parents and left our little rented brownstone before sunrise. We were tired and still emotionally drained from the prior day's events. We arrived in town with about two hours to spare before my speaking event, so we checked into our hotel, I quickly cleaned up, and immediately made my way to the community center the company rented for their annual company-wide gathering.

As I walked up to the front of the building, I noticed a group of roughly twenty-five students, probably middle-schoolers, standing shoulder to shoulder in a semicircle around a flagpole. I stopped for a second to try to figure out what they were doing. That second turned into minutes, and eventually I needed to know, so I walked up to a woman who was standing off to the side and asked. The woman, who was their teacher, shared with me that the election changed the way her students treated one another. They had become more aggressive, racial divides were widening, and she had seen enough. So she had her students stand in the semicircle and asked them to stare at the American flag without saying a word to one another in order to reflect on what it meant to be American.

This teacher was a gift to me, and her students, because I was not in a good place mentally or emotionally to deliver an inspirational keynote. Nothing about me felt inspired at all. But this teacher gave me hope. She let me see that there are good people in the world that are committed to higher morals and values and will do all they can to protect humanity and everything that is good. She inspired me to go inside to do the exact same thing. To remember that it is not about me and to just go be of service, because there were people inside that needed to hear my message. The same message that got me to Dallas.

Inspired by that schoolteacher, I delivered one of the most hope-filled keynotes I have probably ever given. It was as if every word I muttered packed a little extra punch of emotion in it because I knew it had to. The 2016 presidential election not only impacted the behavior of middle-school students, it affected everyone. The campaigning was brutal. The messages were so divisive. And we witnessed the polarization of America that seems to worsen each day.

As I was walking out to my car to head back to my hotel, a young female employee of the company followed me out and asked if we could talk. "Of course," I said. "I'm Matt. It's so nice to meet you." I also remembered her face because throughout my keynote, I'd noticed how emotional she was and how she hung on every word I said.

Looking down at her feet, almost embarrassed or ashamed, she replied, "Hi, my name is Jordan. I want you to know that I believe God brought you here today specifically for me. My plan was to commit suicide tomorrow, and you just saved my life."

I have never had someone approach me and share these words with me before. I was overcome with emotion. Then Jordan said, "I have all the supplies in the trunk of my car to run the exhaust back into the cab of my car and just go to sleep forever. I did a lot of research and this seemed like the best way. But you can have the stuff, because I don't need it anymore."

Oh my. How was I to respond to this? My instinct was to just give Jordan a huge hug and to thank her for having the courage to share this with me, a total stranger to her. I then asked her for permission to have one of the executives of the bank join us for a little conversation. She didn't hesitate for a minute and welcomed my idea.

From that day forward, that executive, myself, my wife, and some of Jordan's team poured constant love on her. Today she is thriving. She has been promoted several times at her company; all the while completing graduate school. Most important, she is happier than she has ever been. Jordan knows how much she matters and is now focused on helping other people know they do too. I believe

Jordan is right: God did have me there that day. God also had her there that day, and I am honored to call Jordan a lifelong friend.

In Dallas, I was the closing speaker for the roughly four hundred women who had gathered at an influencers' meeting. Knowing how challenging it was for me to get on the damn plane, and with my laser focus on being of service, I was committed to delivering a message that the room would remember for a long time. There was just one minor problem: right before I came onstage to close the conference, the emcee took the podium and shared that a freakish snowstorm had just rolled in and they were expecting massive flight cancellations at the airport.

As they drew open the curtains on the floor-to-ceiling windows of the convention room, sure enough, Downtown Dallas was a complete whiteout, and you could hear the collective gasp. Within minutes, the room of four hundred women turned into a room of seventy. It was a mass exodus, and I sat dejected as my audience stormed out of the room. Never the best way to start off a keynote. Once the chaos subsided, the emcee introduced me and I took the stage, only to look out at a room with mostly empty table rounds.

After making a few jokes to calm my nerves and to reconnect the disjointed room, I went straight into my message with the unwavering belief that someone in the room needed to hear my message. After all, that belief is what got me on the plane, and I wasn't going to let that down.

Upon the completion of the keynote, the conference coordinator came onstage to close out the conference and to wish everyone luck getting home in the snow. As I was packing up my belongings, a woman approached me and asked if I had a few minutes to talk. My answer is always yes in moments like this, because I know the person must have something important to share, and I know it probably took some courage to open up to me.

"Hi, Matthew, my name is Mary. I can't thank you enough for your message today, because you helped me embrace how much I matter, but you also opened my eyes to the idea that it isn't all about me."

I thanked Mary and then told her I hoped these new understandings have a lasting positive impact on her life. Mary looked at me and said, "Matthew, they already have." I'm sure Mary noticed the perplexed look on my face, so she continued: "I have been married for almost thirty years. We have three children and have always been the perfect family. But last year I asked for a divorce, and tomorrow we are signing our divorce papers. My decision has torn up our family, and my husband and children don't want us to divorce, but I have been the one pushing it." At this point, I was still a little speechless, because I could tell there was something more she wanted to say.

"Matthew, you just saved our family. As soon as I get to the airport I am calling my kids and my husband to let them know I no longer want a divorce. You made me realize that I was making everything about me. I made myself the victim and blamed him for everything that I didn't like in my life and in our marriage. Now I see so clearly that I was the one causing the hardship. My selfish ways were ruining everything. I can't thank you enough for being here today and for changing my and my family's life."

We hugged, and Mary went on her way to save her family. Which, by the way, she did.

Being of service is not always easy and it's not always convenient. It often requires us to put ourselves second. To reschedule plans. To look up and to be more aware. To conquer our deepest fears. I was scared to death to get back on an airplane. I honestly didn't know if I could ever do it again, but I did. But what if I hadn't been able to get on that first flight to Dallas? We now know that a thirty-year-old marriage would be over and a family torn apart. We also know I would have not been able to fly to Virginia years later, and there is a good chance that Jordan wouldn't be with us anymore. Or what if on that morning in Virginia I didn't shake my mood? What if I had let my anger, confusion, and disappointment keep me from delivering as powerful a message as I could?

If we are truly going to change the world and create a world in which everyone knows how much and why they matter, we all need to show up anyway. It's not always going to be easy, but there is too much at stake if we don't answer the call and step up. We cannot let anything get in the way of serving one another. So always be ready to serve—every day, in every way. Remember, you matter, but it's not always about you.

Pull together a team of friends, family members, colleagues, classmates, or any other sort of group you might be a part of to brainstorm how you, as a team, can be more effective at making a difference in your community. Maybe you can even create a "We Matter" club and commit to being of service once a week or once a month. Consider letting each member pick a different cause each week. It will keep everyone engaged. It will keep things fresh and exciting. Oh, it will probably mean a few folks might face a few fears throughout the year—of course, all in the spirit of team and goodness. All good.

Just remember, as you overcome your fear and take action on it, invite people to join you on the journey or join a group that already exists. This is part of the joy of "we." It applies to both the people we impact and to those we do it with.

What is a fear of yours that keeps you from being of service? Maybe it is volunteering for a cause that might break your heart if you got too close to it. Maybe it is having a tough conversation with someone who really needs help, but you are afraid of how they might react to it. Maybe it means flying all the way around the world to a foreign country to help build water wells or classrooms in a developing country. Well, now is your time to conquer that fear and go for it.

CONVERSATION STARTER

When is a time that you overcame a fear, and how has that impacted you or other people?

12

Be Selfless
GIVE UP YOUR SEAT

If you think you are too small to make a
difference, try sleeping with a mosquito.

—Often attributed to the 14th Dalai Lama

I remember the moment my cell phone rang with an "unknown" number. I was sitting at my desk chair. It was 5:00 P.M. on a Friday, and I was just wrapping up my week. I was nervous. Palms a little sweaty. Because I knew who that "unknown" person was. Well, I didn't know exactly who the person was, but I know where the calling was coming from.

"Hello, this is Matt," I answered, in a bit of a serious tone. Which, for the record, is kind of funny because I am usually not the professional-phone-voice guy.

"Is this Matthew Charles Emerzian?"

"Yes, it is," I confirmed.

"Hi, Matthew, this is Bill from the United States Secret Service, and I have a few questions to ask you. Is that okay with you, sir?" Bill asked.

"Of course it is," I stated firmly.

Then came the barrage: "Where were you born? What was your address in Modesto, California? What are your parents' names? What is your Social Security number?" And the list went on. By the end of the interrogation, I was convinced I was guilty of a crime. I was exhausted.

The call ended with, "Thank you for the information, sir. I just have one more question for you: Are you available at 5:00 A.M. tomorrow morning?" I confirmed that I was, and Bill informed me that I would be hearing back from him in one hour.

An hour later, my phone rang again. Of course, it was my new friend, Bill. "Okay, Matthew. You are cleared. You are now Secret Service level S-9. Here are your instructions: We are going to need you at 5:00 A.M. tomorrow morning. Dressed in a suit and tie. I will call you at 4:00 A.M. with further instructions. We appreciate your service, sir."

I ended the call feeling as though I just accepted my first Mission Impossible. Images of Tom Cruise flashed in front of me. I was committed and there was no turning back now. How did this happen? WTF?

Two years prior to receiving Bill's call, I was flying to Little Rock, Arkansas, to speak at the Clinton School of Public

Service. My flight itinerary required a leg from Los Angeles International Airport to Dallas, Texas, where I had to switch planes for my flight into Little Rock. Much to my surprise, the plane from Dallas to Little Rock was a twelve-seater, which is never a good thing for me. At my size, I could play in the NFL; I am too heavy for most zip lines, and I'd have to enter the Clydesdale division for triathlons. Yes, they really have this division.

As I boarded the plane, crouched over because I couldn't stand up straight without hitting my head, I saw my seat. It was the smallest thing I had ever seen—straight out of kindergarten. It was also the window seat, which meant the curvature of the plane took away half of the vertical space. I tried my best to squeeze into my seat, until I surrendered to the embarrassing truth that I just didn't fit. That's right—I could not fit into my seat on the plane and had to let the flight attendant know.

I figured she would tell me that my only option was to deplane and try to book another flight on a larger plane. But before the stewardess could answer, I heard another passenger comment, "I will happily switch seats with you. My seat has much more room." Her comment caught me off guard because it might have been the first time in recorded history that someone on a flight offered his or her "better" seat to someone else. A bit puzzled, I turned and asked, "Are you sure? I feel bad about that." She replied, "My pleasure."

The flight was a quick one and I was not sitting near her, but I definitely wanted to thank her again and, at a minimum, have a small conversation to acknowledge her kindness.

When we got off the plane in Little Rock, I waited for my co-passenger. As she approached, I quickly shared with her how much I appreciated her gesture and I asked for her name.

She replied, "Hi, my name is Phyllis Dickerson."

"Phyllis Dickerson," I thought. Wow, I love that. Phyllis Dickerson was a beautiful, fashionable, African American businesswoman.

After chatting a little bit, Phyllis Dickerson asked where I was staying and then offered to give me a ride to my hotel.

While driving into town, Phyllis Dickerson and I talked the entire time. It turns out that she worked for the mayor of Little Rock as well as for the Clinton family. She was actually part of the team that had just built the Clinton Presidential Library and the Clinton School of Public Service, so she knew a thing or two about where I was going in Little Rock. She even attended my event the next day, and we have been in contact with each other ever since. A seven-year friendship that began with her offering me her seat on that flight.

But isn't that what life is about? Does it get any simpler than this? Does it need to be any more difficult than this? No, it doesn't. But giving up our seat is not our first inclination. We have to pay extra money now for a good seat on a plane. We cherish and covet that seat with every fiber of our body, as if we own that damn thing. And when we board the plane, we look straight down while everyone else is boarding; we act like we are sleeping, and we hold our breath until the final passenger has boarded and the doors are sealed shut. Why? Because we are praying that no one sits in the seat next to our beloved seat that we paid more money for. I am guilty as charged, but not Phyllis Dickerson. It was more important to her to allow a total stranger to be comfortable. She was happy, I was happy, we were all happy.

At 4:30 P.M., on that same Friday that Bill from Secret Service called me at 5:00 P.M., my phone rang and it was Phyllis Dickerson. For the record, her full name is always one word to me because of how she said it the very first time. See, Phyllis Dickerson is from the Deep South and she has a drawl like none other. She is also a complete character, so just calling her Phyllis is too understated for me.

Our conversation started the same way they always do: "Hey, Phyllis Dickerson, how are you?" Followed by her laughing and saying, "Fine, just fine." Then, Phyllis Dickerson asked me, "Do you have plans tomorrow morning?" I immediately responded, "Why, are you going to be in Los Angeles?" I was excited at the idea of reciprocating her hospitality. "No, I am not going to be there, but a very important person is going to be there, and we need your help."

Attention piqued, I asked, "Who might this very important person be?" Phyllis Dickerson calmly stated, "FLOTUS."

"Matt, our First Lady, Michelle Obama, is coming to L.A., and they are short a driver for her motorcade. Would

you be available for that?" she explained. "If so, a gentleman named 'Bill' is going to call you to see if you clear the
background check. And, if you say yes, you better clear,
because I am the one recommending you."

I hesitated, then replied, "well, let me think if there
is anything they would find. Give me a second." Then,
Phyllis Dickerson said in that perfect southern fashion,
"Riiiiiiiigggggghhhhhhtttttt." Feeling pretty good about
my track record, I told her to count me in. She replied
with, "Great, you will be hearing from Bill in the next few
minutes. Have fun."

Saturday morning came pretty early. I set an alarm for
3:15 and 3:30 A.M. This was not a "mission" I wanted to be
late for. For the record, I have a "Funerals and Weddings
Only" rule when it comes to wearing a suit, so this day was
certainly an exception to the rule. I dusted off my finest
suit, relearned how to get the right length on my tie, and
waited for Bill's call.

At 4:00 A.M. sharp my phone rang and I answered it
right away. "Good morning, sir. Please be at the Beverly
Hills hotel at 5:00 A.M. We will see you shortly." I waited
for a little while, then jumped in my car and headed to the
Beverly Hills Hotel. Everyone knows that hotel in L.A.,
and beyond, because that is the hotel in *Pretty Woman.*

It was still dark when I pulled into the valet parking at
the hotel. In some way, the darkness added to the mystery
of this entire mission. As soon as I stepped out of my car,

who other than Bill himself was there to greet me. Bill was a quintessential Secret Service agent in a dark suit, white collared shirt, tie, badge on his belt, earpiece in his ear with chord wrapping around the back of his neck.

"Hi, Matthew. Thanks for being on time and thanks for your service. Please follow me."

Bill handed me my Secret Service S-9 lapel clip and quickly walked me into the back conference-hall area. We walked up some stairs, down a hall, and into a small room with two sets of doors, then he asked me to wait until he came back with further instructions.

This is the moment that everything started to feel strange. What might have been five minutes felt like thirty. I became convinced that I was in an episode of the TV show *Punk'd,* and I was just waiting for Ashton Kutcher to open one of the sets of doors. I even remember shaking my head and laughing at myself for being such a sucker, and I started to plot how I was going to get Phyllis Dickerson back for this one.

In the middle of my scheming, the back set of doors opened and Bill walked in and closed the door behind him. He sharply stated, "The First Lady would like to personally thank you for your service, but we have one rule: do not ask her any questions or she will talk your ear off, and we are on a tight schedule." I nodded in agreement, but my sarcastic self was thinking, "Oh, okay, Bill. I'll make sure not to ask Ashton any questions. Would hate for him to be late to his next event on a Saturday morning at 5:30."

And then it happened. The door opened again and there stood Michelle Obama, the First Lady of our country, joined by four other Secret Service agents. She immediately walked into the room and looked me right in the eye and said, "I want to thank you so much for helping out today. We truly appreciate it. Would you mind taking a picture together?"

Now, I am not one to get starstruck or uncomfortable with people. Part of this is because I have worked with so many celebrities, coupled with the fact that I really just try to see people for who they are on the inside. But this was completely different.

To begin with, Michelle Obama is strikingly beautiful. Tall. Her eyes are so engaging and her smile is infectious. And from the first moment I saw her, I understood what Bill meant about talking my ear off, because she engages so quickly. Instantly present and genuinely interested. I was absolutely starstruck.

To this day, I don't remember a single word I said back to her. They may not have even been words—rather, some sort of mumbling. It was one of those moments when all of the internal wiring just short-circuits and, at best, I might have resembled C-3PO from *Star Wars*.

The moment lasted two minutes, tops. We talked about something, took a photo, shared a smile, and off they took her. Like a puff of smoke. Gone. Vanished.

Immediately after, Bill kicked into mission mode. "Okay Matthew, here is the plan. . . . We are going to start bringing down all of the luggage, and your job is to load it into your van and drive it to LAX with another one of our agents. So please head outside and stand by the van."

As I stood on my mark, they began wheeling out the hotel luggage racks, loaded with black suitcases and garment bags. The first bag I grabbed was a hanging bag, and while transferring it to the van, I saw it . . . the official United States presidential luggage tag that read FLOTUS. "Holy crap, I am literally carrying the First Lady's luggage right now. This is awesome. This is crazy. I better not mess this up." We quickly loaded the van with all of the bags from her entire team and headed off to the airport.

Unbeknownst to me, LAX has a special back entrance, reserved just for people like POTUS and FLOTUS. As you can imagine, this entrance is well equipped with security measures. After passing through the protocol, we drove onto the tarmac to be welcomed by another team of Secret Service agents, all standing in front of FLOTUS's plane. The plane was snow-white front to back, top to bottom, with just a few small American flag decals on it. Understated yet dignified.

Our first order was to remove all the luggage from the van and to spread it out on the tarmac in a grid, with roughly three feet between each bag. After completing our grid, which was probably fifty feet by fifty feet, we were asked to step aside. Next order of business was to bring out the dog, and we stood and watched as a Secret Service member circled each and every bag, with the dog sniffing away at every angle.

As soon as the dog completed his round of security, a

mobile luggage-security machine was driven out on the tarmac right up to the belly of the plane. One by one, we put the bags through the machine. As the bags came out the other side of the machine, they were immediately loaded into the luggage compartment on the belly of the plane, until the very last bag was in.

We were done. Mission accomplished. I was spent and struggling to process the entire sequence of events. The agent whom I accompanied in the van then came to me with the next instructions: "Matthew, I am going to stay here with the plane, so we need you to drive back to the hotel with the van. Does that work for you, sir?" With a quick "Absolutely," I jumped into my van and headed off the tarmac and out of LAX.

Only two minutes into my drive back to the hotel, my phone rang. It was Bill again. Hurriedly, Bill asked, "How many minutes until you are back to the hotel with the van? We need you back immediately. Hurry, but be safe. Thanks." Just when I thought my nerves could take a break, it was "Game On" again and I was flying my van down the freeway in hot pursuit of the hotel.

As I pulled into the valet area for the second time that morning, once again I was greeted by Bill. "Thank you for getting here so quickly, sir. We now need you again, if that is okay with you." What was I going to say? No? "Of course, Bill, what do you need?" Mission Impossible II, here we go.

"You are going to drive one of the vans in the motorcade back to LAX," Bill ordered.

"You mean, I am in one of the vans or actually driving one?" I asked.

"Driving, sir," Bill said. "Come with me and I will show you to your new van."

Bill and I walked around to the side of the hotel toward the back alley. Sitting there were three vans, two Suburbans, and roughly twelve motorcycle officers.

"Matt, this is your van and here are your keys. Please get in the driver's seat now, put on your seat belt, check your mirrors, and start the engine," Bill explained. "We will be leaving in a minute."

If I was ever going to have an Indy 500 moment in my life, this was it. Mirrors checked, seat belt on, engine running, hands clutching the wheel at 10:00 and 2:00, knuckles white, palms sweating, adrenaline pumping. OMG. I was ready.

Without a moment to reconsider, my passenger door opened and I was greeted by yet another Secret Service agent. I asked him if there were any special instructions and explained that I had never done this before. He said, "Just stay within a car length of the van in front of you, and don't stop until we are at the plane. That's it."

I replied, "What if something bad happens? What do I do?"

To which he calmly replied, "Don't worry about that. See those two Suburbans? They will take care of any possible problem before you even have time to exhale."

Under my breath, I mumbled, "Got it."

He looked at me and said, "Get ready, here we go." On

cue, the back passenger doors opened, and next thing I knew, my van had six people in it. The doors shut. The van in front of me started to move, and once again it was "Go Time."

I didn't say a single word for the first five minutes of our drive. I was in the zone, as if playing a driving video game. The roads were being cleared and the intersections blocked by the motorcycle patrol, and we were driving over 50 mph down the streets of L.A.—flanked by the Suburbans with men and large guns.

Right as we were pulling onto the 405 freeway, which was also closed down to all traffic, I felt a slight tickle on the back of my neck as if someone were playing with my hair. Not wanting to take my hands off the steering wheel, I just tried to ignore it. But then I felt it again, and from the gentleman sitting right behind me, I heard, "Well, what's our driver's name? He sure has beautiful hair."

I looked over at the Secret Service agent sitting next to me to visibly get his approval for me to reply.

"My name is Matt. It's nice to meet you. I have never done this before, so I am a little tense right now," I admitted.

Then the passenger replied, "Well it's sure nice to meet you, Matthew. You are doing a great job. And I just love your hair. I would love to work on it sometime. Those curls are just amazing."

Trying to be friendly, but still a bit dry, I asked, "Oh, are you a hairstylist?"

He responded, "Yes, we are Michelle's beauty team—hair, makeup, fashion."

"So, Mr. Matthew, what do you do for a living?" he asked.

"I wrote a book called *Every Monday Matters,* and now do a lot of speaking and writing and I run our organization," I shared.

"And what is the book about?" he followed up.

I quickly explained it to him, but the truth is that I just wanted to end the conversation. At that point, we were driving 80 mph down the freeway, and I had to stay within one car length from the car in front of me. Anything to stop him from talking to me so I could focus was a good thing to me.

"Well, Mr. Matthew, we would all love a copy of your book," he shared. "Would you also sign it for us?"

Instantly, I grabbed my cell phone and handed it over my right shoulder without taking my eyes off the road. "Of course I would. Just enter your information into my phone, and I will send you signed copies," I said. I really thought that was going to be the break I needed, but I was quickly mistaken.

"Umm, Mr. Matthew, what is your code to get into your phone?" he asked.

"Oh, sorry. It's . . ." Before finishing my sentence I knew exactly what was about to happen, and it was not going to go well. With no turning back, I finished, ". . . 6-9-6-9. I was born in 1969." Then I waited . . . for a millisecond.

"Oh, I like our driver even more now. I see how you are, Mr. Every Monday Matters Matthew. You are fun,

Mr. Sixty-Nine, Sixty-Nine," he shared loudly for the entire van to enjoy.

At that moment I looked back at my copilot, Mr. Secret Service agent, and, for the first time he cracked a smile and shook his head. I couldn't help but start laughing, and next thing you know, the entire van was cracking up. Somehow this insanely intense situation became a mini road trip with friends. This group was a blast, and for the first time that day I actually started to enjoy myself.

As we pulled back onto the same tarmac I visited on my first mission, the team jumped out. He yelled, "We love you, Mr. Matthew. Thank you," and off they went. I sat in my van and watched all three vans unload their passengers. Then, there she was—FLOTUS. Smiling and waving and thanking everyone.

They quickly boarded the plane, the door was sealed, the plane pulled away, and within seven minutes, per their protocol, the wheels were off the ground and they were gone.

I stepped out of my van and looked for Bill. Everyone was relaxed and chatting away. It was as if they had just removed their costumes and let their hair down. Their work was finished. As I walked up to him with a smile of relief, he turned and looked at me and said, "Great job, Matt. Honestly, you were great. If you don't mind, we would like to add you to our list for upcoming situations. You should see what it is like when POTUS is here."

What was I going to say?

*   *   *

Patty and I are both fans of Shonda Rhimes's book *Year of Yes*. No doubt it is a great one and my wife refers to it all the time. At the same time, and not to say that Shonda Rhimes would disagree with me on this, I am also a believer in boundaries. As someone who suffered from anxiety, I know the negative impact of not having healthy boundaries in your life. Anxiety disorder is often referred to as "The Nice Person's Disease." Lovely.

But there is something in all of this that makes me believe that life unfolds based on our willingness to just show up and get in the game. Life is both beautiful and messy, and either way, we need to show up for it. I had never suffered from anxiety disorder or chronic depression before, but once I did, I had to put in the work to fix it. I had never written a book before, but once I had the idea, I wrote it. I was never trained to be a public speaker and certainly never thought I would air my dirty laundry in front of thousands of people on stages across America, but I have, and it has changed lives. And I was certainly never a Secret Service agent or a driver for FLOTUS's motorcade, but once I got the call, I served.

I believe this is exactly what Phyllis Dickerson did. She saw a complete stranger struggling with his seat on the plane, and she stepped in and stepped up and made the gesture. Over the years, I have learned that this is just who Phyllis Dickerson is. She is a team player. A giver. She is not afraid of challenges and loves life. Her attitude is contagious; her commitment to her community, and even strangers, makes a difference. Phyllis Dickerson makes life better for everyone and anyone around her because she is committed to it. I benefited from it before I could even call her "friend." What if, instead of saying yes to my little situation on the plane, she had just looked the other way with a "no, not my problem" attitude?

Too many of us are waiting to be asked instead of being the ones who ask. We stand on the sidelines and either watch life go by or see ourselves as victims of it. But what would our world, and all of our lives, look like if we just did what Phyllis Dickerson did? Remember, all she did was give up her seat, but my life has been blessed over and over because of it.

Because of her, I was able to make that flight and have the honor of speaking at the Clinton School of Public Service. Because of her, I am now an S-9 Secret Service agent. Because of her, I met and served First Lady Michelle Obama. And, because of her, I now have an amazing and inspirational friend for life.

It's amazing how acts of selflessness can ripple out in ways we can never predict.

Mission accomplished.

TAKE ACTION

The smallest of gestures can have lasting and significant impact on people and the world. Commit to doing one small gesture of selflessness every day for the rest of your life. Yes,

I said, "for the rest of your life." That's 365 times many, many years, I hope. What a way to live. What a legacy to create. Make sure to include your friends or family members as well. Now the numbers are getting up there. . . . This is how we do it.

JOURNAL PROMPT

A friend of mine once said that acts of selflessness are truly just selfish in nature, because people do them to feel good about themselves. I disagreed with him. While it's highly possible to feel good internally as a by-product of acting selflessly, I don't believe that is the intention of the initial gesture of selflessness. But then I flipped it around and said, "Fine. Then let's create the most selfish world we have ever seen, and see where that gets us." What are your thoughts about his statement?

CONVERSATION STARTER

When is a time that you have benefited directly or indirectly from the actions of a total stranger?

13

Be Honest
SEE THE INVISIBLE

Waking up this morning, I smile.

Twenty-four brand new hours are
before me.

I vow to live fully in each moment

and to look at all beings with eyes of
compassion.

—Thich Nhat Hanh

My mind raced at a million thoughts per second. Every part of me thought this was the right thing to do, but in this moment, I began to question myself. Maybe it was the chain-link-fence tunnel we were walking through. Maybe it was the rolls of barbed wire seemingly strewn everywhere.

Or maybe it was the holding cells we stumbled upon, where we stood and waited for one door to close before the next one would open, clearly controlled by someone somewhere watching us on a monitor. With every step in, it became harder to get out. But isn't that the point of prison?

The difference on this day is that I *chose* to be there. Sure, one might argue that everyone in prison chose that for him- or herself, be it the employees or the incarcerated. But I hadn't committed a crime, and I was not on payroll. I also had Patty with me, which added an extra layer of angst. But I was there because I received a letter from an inmate that moved me to tears and put a calling on my heart to go.

Seven months prior to this day, I was in Olympia, Washington, to speak at an event hosted by the secretary of state. It was a true honor to be selected, to get a private tour of the breathtaking and majestic capitol building, and to sit in the secretary of state's office with her and her amazing team. I felt like the man of the hour. I guess in some ways I was.

The intention of this event was to kick off the Washington State Combined Fund Drive. This is an annual drive that provides state employees the opportunity to donate resources to nonprofit organizations all across the state. I am talking about millions of dollars that are used to make a big impact. Yes, this means I was there to get everyone pumped up to give again . . . and not just the same as they gave in previous years, but even more. No pressure.

Big events like this often use cameras to get close-ups on the speaker in order to project a video on large screens to the left and right of the stage. We have all seen this before at concerts, sporting events, and yes, even stately breakfasts. In this case, however, in addition to projecting a larger image of me onto screens, unbeknownst to me, these cameras were also recording my keynote. Also, unbeknownst to me, my keynote would eventually make its way onto TVW, Washington's public affairs television network, which happens to air in Washington's prison system, of all places.

A few months after the event was over, I received a piece of mail with the return address of Stafford Creek Corrections Center. My address and the return address were both handwritten and not in the most professional penmanship. The return address also included the name "Chris" with a serial number next to his name. I curiously wondered who this was, why I was receiving it, and what was inside the envelope.

What I discovered inside was one of the sweetest, most generous, and authentic letters I have ever read. On six pages of lined binder paper, the letter was handwritten with a blue ballpoint pen, front and back. It was in Chris's letter where I learned my keynote was recorded and aired on TVW. It was also Chris's words, emotions, and details that started my eye-opening and overwhelming journey into the world of incarceration—one that continues to this very day.

Chris shared with me that if he had known or felt like he

mattered, he probably would have made different choices in life. In other words, he wouldn't be in prison. He asked me to come to Stafford Creek to talk to a roomful of inmates. Why? Not for his sake; he is in for life. He wanted his fellow inmates that didn't have life sentences to hear my message in the hope that when they got out of prison my words would keep them from returning. If that wasn't selfless and special enough already, he also offered to pay for it by going on a payment plan with me, even though he only makes fifty dollars a week, working full-time.

This is why, just a few months later, Patty and I, along with Philip from the secretary of state's office, entered Stafford Creek Corrections Center. Not on Chris's dime, but mine. I had to go.

We live in very interesting times today. Might I even say conflicted and destructive times? "We" is no longer the universal "we" that includes all of us. We have division. We see difference as bad. We judge. We bully. We are either a Republican or Democrat, black or white, gay or straight, fat or fit. Everything has a label. A category. And these labels have become the driving forces for our beliefs, our actions, our words, and our character.

We no longer see our most important label as "Human." Nope. Because if we did, we would see more love, kindness, compassion, empathy, faith, selflessness, encouragement, friendship, loving families, good neighbors, and role models. Of course, this would happen only if we believe this is what it means to be human in the first place. I believe it is, but we just do a really lousy job of remembering it.

Instead, I see political affiliations break apart friendships and families, as "blue" or "red" means more than love and connection. I see religion judging others, completely void of understanding, empathy, and care, only seeing "sinners" that aren't living the "right" way, at least according to them. I watch people walk semicircles around homeless people, as if to say, "How dare you make me walk around you?" And we have all watched racism and sexism flourish in the past few years, just when we thought we were becoming a more self- and socially aware society. And in all of this divided, ego-driven, right-and-wrong way of thinking, we have become splintered.

But then something happens. Something that calls us back to our deepest nature. Something that allows us to remember that we can thrive and do better . . . together. Throw our broken "we" a hurricane, a flood, a fire, a humanitarian crisis, and just watch how we rise up and come together. The labels that divide us all go away. We are no longer white, brown, or black. We are no longer gay or straight or transgender. Christian or Jew or Muslim. In these moments we become human again—loving, kind, compassionate, empathetic, caring, and so on. In all of the tragedy, a beautiful tale is told of people coming together to achieve the impossible, and we see the human spirit sing louder than ever.

But then something happens again. The waters disperse, the last flames are extinguished, and the news cycle moves on . . . and so does our human nature. No sooner are we our best, than we slide back into our worst . . . until the next big disaster.

This cycle brings hope for humanity, but it also shows our brokenness and our inability to see the inconvenient truth. For there are invisible tragedies happening every single day that we fail to see because they are not headline news. Every day in America, twenty veterans commit suicide, but we don't see it. But if every week for a year the headline read ANOTHER COMMERCIAL PLANE FILLED WITH VETERANS CRASHED, it would get our attention.

What about our senior population that is growing in number, isolated and depressed, dying alone in senior homes? What about the over half a million homeless men, women, and children sleeping and starving in America on any given night? There are abandoned animals that need homes, children who need school supplies, beaches and rivers that need cleaning, victims of domestic violence, adults that can't read, families that can't afford funeral services for a loved one.

The ugly truth that we don't like to see is that we are surrounded by tragedy every single day. The uglier truth is that most of us are not doing anything about it. Instead we turn the other cheek and go about our merry way as if "it's not my problem." When it comes to "we" there is no such thing as "It's not my problem." Because "we" doesn't include "me" and "him" or "us" and "them." We are the "we."

But living and seeing life this way requires much of us.

It means going out of our way. It means learning things we will never unlearn. It means having our hearts broken. It means changing our "only want to feel good" ways to be of service to others, even when it hurts. It means seeing the invisible all around us. Welcome to the gates of Stafford Creek.

We eventually arrived at the door to the prison lunchroom and, one by one, we walked into the room. The room was perfectly square, probably one hundred feet by one hundred feet, with table rounds gathered in the middle. Prison guards and vending machines lined the sterile walls around the tables, leaving a ten-foot moat between the walls and the first convicts. All two hundred seats were filled with gentlemen wearing their best prison fashion, sitting in anticipation of me. All I needed to do was summon the courage to walk out in front of the room to the lonely podium awaiting my arrival.

These men did not know who I was, and they didn't know why I was there. Not even Chris. I walked up to the podium, looked at the longing faces that filled the room, and began reading Chris's letter. I was in. No turning back now. Magically, the next two hours were filled with laughter, tears, purpose, significance, love, kindness, courage, friendship, and family. We were all being human.

Most important for me, is that I believe these men finally got a hint of knowing and understanding that their lives still mattered and it wasn't too late to live a life filled with purpose and significance. I watched them sit taller, engage with each other, put down their prisoner persona to be vulnerable and authentic and to own their actions. But, selfishly and equally important to me, this day changed me, too.

That day, I chose to fly three hours, then drive another three hours to see the invisible. I had never entered a prison before. I had never stood in front of two hundred murderers, rapists, thieves, and drug dealers. In my naïveté and prejudice, people who committed crimes were "not my problem" and deserved all the punishment they received and more. They messed up, so they should pay the price. I made myself the judge and the jury for every single juvenile delinquent and adult criminal. But on that day at Stafford Creek, it all changed.

This is what seeing the invisible does. It changes you . . . for the better. It helps you grow to be a better human, for it pulls the love and compassion and empathy out of you. I stopped seeing a convicted murderer. Instead I started seeing a young twenty-one-year-old who never had a father and was beat up daily by his mom's boyfriend. I stopped seeing a gang member. Instead I started seeing a young nineteen-year-old boy who grew up homeless without any sense of belonging or identity and found family and connection and meaning in a gang. In so many of these cases, I found that they were paying the punishment for crimes committed before they were even born. That their bad choices were part of a series of bad choices that came before them. This is not to excuse them for what they did, for they don't want the excuses, either; rather, it is just to better understand who these people are as part of our collective "we," whether we want to acknowledge that or not.

A few weeks after that magical day at Stafford Creek, I received another letter from Chris. Besides thanking me for surprising him, he wanted to share a moment with me that meant the world to him. After I finished speaking to the group, Chris came over to officially introduce himself to me. I spoke with him for a little bit and then introduced him to Patty before being pulled away to meet other inmates. This was the special moment Chris was referring to. He wrote, "Your wife gave me a hug and told me that I was 'good stuff,' and you showed that you trusted me. A convicted murderer. You trusted me to speak with the most important person in your life without watching over me, and I can't thank you enough for that."

As I read his letter, I realized he was right. I didn't see Chris as a murderer. I saw him as another person. A human. Just like me. That was the only label present. And, without knowing who he was or what he had done, Patty told him he was "good stuff." How beautiful is that?

Chris has since been transferred to another location, but I made another friend that day at Stafford Creek as well. His name is Matt. We speak on the phone weekly. Matt has already served eighteen years for murder and has another seventeen years left. He was nineteen when he committed his crime. Matt is one of the kindest, most loving, and inspirational friends that I have today. That is saying a lot because I have a lot of amazing friends. But just like I am different today than I was eighteen years ago, so is Matt. Today he leads restorative-justice programs at Stafford Creek, and upon his release he wants to work together to bring a message of hope, purpose, and mattering to prisons nationwide.

Matt has made me a better person. Stafford Creek has made me a better person. Chris's letters have made me a better person. They would have done the same for you. Whether we want to embrace it or not, our culture, our society is made up of a little bit of everything. This includes everyone, not just folks that fit our image or mold of what people should be. After all, if we are kind and bold enough to acknowledge it, don't we all have a bit of brokenness in us? Just one of the many things we share in common.

So what is the invisible that you have avoided seeing? It's time for all of us to truly start seeing life as a "we" thing, because we are all part of that "we." Together, we will become better people and create a better world.

TAKE ACTION

When you commit to seeing the world as a "we" thing, you realize the interconnectedness of all of us. This doesn't mean that we don't see difference, because there is beauty in our differences. This is part of the stunning mosaic of life—the blend of cultures, beliefs, foods, lands, music, and more. But be honest with yourself here: What is a judgment or a prejudice you may have that has kept you from being of service toward a specific need or people? Maybe it is that homeless people are worthless and annoying and it's their choice to be that way. Maybe, like me, it is that kids in juvenile hall deserve to be there. Maybe people suffering from drug addiction have no one else to blame but themselves. Pick your prejudice, then choose to be kind. Choose to learn more, to be willing to better understand, and to serve. Remember, these "invisible" people want to feel like they matter, too. Just like the rest of us.

JOURNAL PROMPT

It is really easy for us to complain about our community or our culture. I see it all the time, especially in companies and organizations. People love to say how terrible their corporate culture is, so I always respond with, "What are you doing to change it?" See, each one of us is an integral part of several communities and cultures. I am part of my company's culture. Why? Because I work there. It's not as if the culture is over there and I am over here. No. I am it and it is me. The same goes for my neighborhood, my family, my tennis club, my city. We all need to take equal responsibility for creating the type of communities and cultures we want to have.

So make a list of the different cultures and communities that you play a role in. Then write down three ways you are going to make a positive impact on each of them. While you are at it, share your plan with other people in each of your respective communities and ask them to do the same thing. This is how we change things on a bigger level.

CONVERSATION STARTER

What is one thing you hate about your community? Great. What are you doing to change it?

14

Be Generous
BE GRATEFUL AND GIVING

For it is in giving that we receive.

—St. Francis of Assisi

My wife's favorite two living souls to ever walk the face of the earth are her father and one of our three rescue kitties, Rooster. I feel fairly secure in my third position and just embrace the fact that not all battles need to be fought. Sadly, her father, Victor, passed away eighteen years ago, before she and I met. It would have been nice to meet my wife's #1, but I also feel like I know him in so many ways.

Victor loved his family, especially Patty. She was the youngest, therefore always the baby. She also got her dad's big ears and terrible vision, meaning, like her father, she wore thick-lensed glasses at a young age. He was a sailor and served in the military, working on aircraft carriers. Small in stature but scrappy as hell with his Irish and Scottish blood pumping through his veins. As beautiful and sweet as my wife is, coupled with the smallest fists you have ever seen, she also has her fair share of piss and vinegar in her. Whenever I tell people this, they never believe me. I always get, "Patty? No way. She's the sweetest person ever." It's true.

Like her father, Patty got in a ton of fights growing up. It started by being bullied for having big ears, thick glasses, and being a skinny little beanpole. But kids quickly learned her fearless ways and the power of her tiny little fists. As she got older, she became sensitive to other people who were bullied and became their protector, punching bullies in the face on a regular basis. Each occurrence led to a parent-teacher conference, where her father said, "Well, sounds like they deserved what they got." A proud papa for sure. Thankfully she doesn't punch people anymore, and she uses her "voice for the voiceless" calling to protect animals—hence being a vegan, and Rooster being #2.

But there was one thing about her #1 that drove her nuts. Victor gave away everything. At any given moment that Patty would ask her father if he had seen something, he would reply, "Oh, I gave that to this boy down the street," or "You know, your Uncle Kenny needed it for something he was working on." One day, while Patty waited in the car when her dad was in a store, he came walking out in just a T-shirt—but he'd walked in wearing a sweatshirt. "Dad, where is your sweatshirt?" she asked. "Well, Patty, this kid

in there needed it more than I did." Literally the sweatshirt off his back. I love that.

I find this characteristic so special for so many reasons. First of all, the Malcolm family didn't have a lot to give away in the first place. They certainly weren't poor, by any means, but it's not like they had two of everything, either. But second, I believe Mr. Malcolm got so much joy in giving that it lit him up. He was both grateful and giving, and this was part of the blessing he was to his community. He was a sweet little man who went around town look-ing for opportunities to give; I wish I could have witnessed it with my own eyes.

The irony of all this is that Patty happened to marry someone just like her #1—me, #3. No, I'm not small and scrappy. Quite the opposite. No, I am not a fighter. Never punched a single person in my life. But giving and gener-ous? Absolutely. And my poor wife still asks the same ques-tions and hears the same answer: "Babe, our housekeeper, Martha, really liked it, so I gave it to her." "Babe, I met this kid in the store and . . ."

But I can't take credit for being generous, because it was something I learned the easy way. I remember my grand-father driving around Fresno in his El Camino loaded with apple boxes to give to his friends, family, and even strangers. I remember my grandmother telling a home-less man sleeping on the bench at a bus stop to wait for her to come back with dinner for him—a home-cooked din-ner that she poured tons of time and love into. This gener-osity rubbed off on the next generation of Emerzians and

Matoians. My uncles are still giving to us younger generation and to their community. My father served on countless non-profit boards and gave his time, talent, and treasure to his family and community. My mother has constantly looked for places to be of service and has cooked and delivered food to many families and friends dealing with illness or loss. She's also famous for slipping me and my brother a twenty-dollar bill or two and saying, "Shhhh, don't tell your father." Even though he always knew and was just fine with it.

Patty and I got married on August 10, 2013. It was the most beautiful wedding and special day of our lives. Thanks to the generosity of the Gallo family, we got married at Bridle-wood Vineyards in Santa Ynez, California. The year 2013 was also when I decided to flip Every Monday Matters from a for-profit company to a not-for-profit organization, meaning it was financially a tough year. Day one as a not-for-profit usually means zero donors—start-up not-for-profits don't typically get people throwing their money at them. But because of my father's forty-seven years at E. & J. Gallo Winery, the employee-engagement work we were doing with Gallo through Every Monday Matters, and the lifelong friendship we have developed with the Gallo family, we were offered any of their vineyards for our wedding venue at no cost to us. Oh, that included the wine, too. So kind, and quite the upgrade from the back-yard wedding we realistically had in mind.

We couldn't go on a honeymoon right away, as we

needed to save up enough money first; but three years later, we went on the honeymoon of our dreams to the Guanacaste region of Costa Rica. Patty found an incredible home on VRBO owned by our (now) good friends, Sam and Mary, and we spent eight days watching monkeys in our backyard trees, floating in our infinity pool that dropped into the Pacific Ocean, zip-lining, riding quads, driving through rivers, swimming in the crystal-clear ocean, and witnessing the invasion of thousands of olive ridley turtles as they floated onshore to lay their eggs—a moment we will never forget.

As thrilling and breathtaking as everything was that we did in Costa Rica, the most meaningful part of our trip was meeting Yorjani and Maureen, a young local couple in their late twenties who managed Sam and Mary's home as well as a few other properties on the finca (farm). What's incredible about this finca is that the homes are all straight out of *Architectural Digest,* but in the middle of absolutely nowhere. To get to the house, we had to drive two and a half hours from the airport, with the final hour of the trip on a bumpy, gutted-out dirt road. To make matters worse, there are no streetlights, so it was pitch-black and dusty. We had to drive through multiple rivers, and our brains were thoroughly mush from the sixty minutes of rattling and bumps. I remember saying to Patty, "I think this is where people like Jason Bourne, from the movie *Bourne Identity,* go to retire so no one ever finds them again."

This is also where Yorjani and Maureen were born and grew up. Not inside the fenced-in architectural majesty of the finca with its 180-degree views of the Pacific Ocean, but in the tiny cinder-block, blue-tarp fishing village of San Juanillo, population two hundred on a crowded day. Yorjani's mom did everything she could to provide for her large family. She sold ceviche, shrimp, and lobster tails, depending on the morning's catch. She sold motorcycle fuel, which she poured out of old laundry detergent bottles. Seeing families of four on a single motorcycle was an hourly occurrence. Yorjani's sister was a cook at a tiny local restaurant. And Yorjani and Maureen managed properties, meaning they welcomed guests, removed iguanas from attics, cleaned floor-to-ceiling, and fixed anything broken. Both of their families operated by the "it takes a village" mentality, and it worked perfectly. They lived comfortably, for Costa Rican standards—easy on the material riches but overflowing with love, joy, and *Pura vida*.

We quickly fell in love with Yorjani, Maureen, and their families. We had them all up to the house for dinner, spent hours each day adventuring together, and truly immersed ourselves in the way they do life. Simple. Pure. Loving. Refreshing.

One evening, while were sitting by our pool, Patty asked Yorjani and Maureen if they ever planned on or talked about getting married. They had been dating for years and were such a cute couple that clearly we thought it was time. The fact that it was our honeymoon also added some extra courage for us to pry deeper. Yorjani sheepishly explained that they weren't in a rush, because they couldn't afford the wedding they hoped to have one day.

Clearly, we understood this reality, but we also encouraged them to just move into it and to let the universe provide. It worked for us. We also reassured them that whatever their wedding would be, it would be perfect. In other words, don't wait.

Then, Patty made an unbelievably beautiful gesture. She looked into Maureen's big almond-shaped eyes and said, "Maureen, when you are ready, you can have my wedding dress, if you would like it." Instantly, both Patty and Maureen started to cry tears of joy, as they sweetly hugged. Yorjani, a bit stunned and choked up, realized their wedding just got one step closer, and all of us celebrated the kindness of Patty's gesture and the inevitability of their wedding.

We left Costa Rica the next day but promised to return soon. We now had family there, and we missed them immediately after a tearful goodbye, checking out of the house, and handing over the keys.

We came home from Costa Rica and we were on fire. Patty might as well have taken a job at the official Costa Rica Tourism Board. If you came anywhere within her vicinity or followed her on social media, you would get an ear- and eyeful of Costa Rica. She was hooked and also developed a super-meaningful relationship with Maureen. Two women, worlds apart with a major language barrier, building a friendship like none I've ever seen Patty connect with.

I told Patty that her offering to Maureen was one of the sweetest gestures I have ever seen anyone make in my life.

In that moment, Patty gave this young couple hope. She showed them such deep love and support, and the glow on Maureen's face was absolutely priceless. Because Patty works in television in America, she was quite the hit in Costa Rica. We joked that she has a huge acting career and fan base in San Juanillo. Plus, Patty is stunningly beautiful and was even more so in her wedding dress on our special day. I think Maureen was also a little starstruck by Patty, which only added to the allure and excitement of wearing her wedding dress. So sweet.

Patty said to me, "Babe, I wore that dress on the biggest day of my life, and we had the dream wedding because of the generosity of other people. I wanted to pay that forward in some small way, and I want Maureen to feel just as happy and beautiful on her wedding day as I did. I didn't even think twice about it."

To this day, I am still so proud and in love with what Patty did. It has also become great ammunition for me to say, "Hey, babe, have you seen your wedding dress laying around lately?" when she discovers I have given something else away. Only to hear her say, "No honey, I met this girl in Costa Rica and wanted her to have it for her special day."

A few months passed by while Patty and Maureen continued to build their friendship, and then my dad surprised us by sharing that he wanted to celebrate his eightieth birthday with a family vacation in Costa Rica. Patty especially was elated . . . she is clearly a great sales person. We couldn't wait to see our Costa Rican family again and to show our own family this very special place on our planet.

A week before leaving for my dad's eightieth in Costa Rica, we received a video call from Maureen. Patty and I were just relaxing at home eating dinner and enjoying a glass of wine when the call came through. Patty quickly answered the phone, and there they were—Maureen and Yorjani showing us Maureen's new ring and screaming, "We did it. We are engaged!" Patty and I jumped up from the table in celebration, and the four of us rejoiced over video. I truly believe that Patty's offering put all of this into motion. I was so proud and so happy—one of those type of special moments in life that we all need to savor more often.

This also meant something else though: it was time to pack the wedding dress, because it was coming with us to Costa Rica.

Patty and I flew down to Costa Rica with my mom and dad. My brother and his wife and kids were coming down the day after us, which meant we reserved two large SUVs. Always book a 4WD in Costa Rica. The four of us landed, gathered our luggage, then took a shuttle to the car-rental location.

While my mom and Patty watched the luggage and the dress, my dad and I processed the car rental, only to discover they no longer had large SUVs. Trouble. Between the four of us, we had four large suitcases, four carry-ons, and one wedding dress that was professionally cleaned and sealed in a large box that was bigger than our suitcases. A midsize SUV could never handle everything we packed. Sure enough, I was right. Everything fit except the dress.

In true Costa Rica fashion, the gentleman at the counter said, "No problem, we will pay for a taxi to follow you with the wedding dress." This meant a poor taxi driver had to drive two and a half hours on a bumpy dirt road, through rivers, in the pitch black, while eating our dust behind our car to get to the house . . . with the dress. "*Pura vida,*" they said. "It's okay." Off we went—the four of us and our luggage in one car, the wedding dress by itself behind us, like a hearse of joy.

Thankfully, all of our family and the wedding dress made it safely to the finca, and we planned a special evening for Maureen and Yorjani to come get the dress. There was a stunning Costa Rican sunset, as most of them seem to be. We were all lounging by the pool in the backyard, looking over the jungle and Río Nosara, listening to the birds and the monkeys in surround sound, and gazing out at the vast ocean, as the sky was ablaze with orange, yellow, red, and magenta. With champagne in hand and "Here Comes the Bride" playing in the background, Patty walked the wedding dress box out for Maureen to unwrap and hold for the first time. The dress had officially been passed to its new rightful owner and she was overwhelmed with emotion. We all smiled, cried, celebrated, and toasted the soon-to-be bride and groom.

This act of generosity and story of love and friendship were a year in the making. It's pretty awesome to think back on that special evening when Patty first offered Maureen her dress. But the story doesn't end there. Maureen and Yorjani shared with all of us that they had set a date for their wedding for December, just four months away. And within moments of holding her dress, Maureen and Yorjani gave us an even bigger gift—the privilege of being the official witnesses of their marriage. So special.

Four months later, Patty and I found ourselves back in Costa Rica to celebrate the marriage of Yorjani and Maureen. They honored us by having us be part of the ceremony and to sit at the family table during the reception. They even informed us, ten minutes before the wedding started, that we were the best man and matron of honor. But it would be a little tricky to give a speech that no one would understand. Maureen glowed as she walked down the aisle in Patty's former dress. She even had Patty do her hair and makeup, so the similarities were striking. Yorjani stood at the front of the altar as Maureen made her way to him. He then turned his head to look at me and Patty, smiled, and mouthed, "Whoa!"

It is hard to put the emotions into words, but every single part of it was perfect. Friends for life, bound by the sweetest gesture and a wedding dress. *Pura vida.*

What do you have that you are holding on to so tightly but would be a true treasure for someone else? It doesn't have to be as sentimental as your wedding dress, though I can make a pretty good argument why it could be. What about shoes, purses, business suits, furniture, baby cribs, older cell phones, televisions? Our inclination is to hold on to everything. We would rather pay one hundred dollars a month to store it somewhere, where we know we will never see it again, than to give it to someone or a family that will love and cherish it. Be grateful for what you have, but be even more inspired to give it away.

At the same time, I often reflect on experiences like "Operation Wedding Dress," and I think about all of the things that needed to take place in order for the story to unfold. The days, weeks, months, and years. All of the people or characters in the story. The different meaningful events and locations. The different languages and countries. And mostly the generosity that laid the foundation for all of it. This is a story of giving from start to finish, and we are so grateful for it.

When we all show up in a grateful and giving way, we help dreams come true for one another, and that's a life well lived and a world well served.

TAKE ACTION

When is the last time you went through your closet and took an honest inventory of how much stuff you have but don't need or use? If you have done this recently, nice work. Now do the same thing in your garage. If you haven't done this recently, now is your time to do so. Create rules for yourself before starting. For example: "If I haven't worn it in the past six months, it must go." Or: "I have more than two of a particular item, then one must go." Sorry ladies, five pair of black boots and eight purses just aren't necessary. But you make your own rules, so I will shut up now. With your rules in place, get to cleaning. Remember, your closet is full of items that would be absolute treasures for someone.

One of the most amazing things about seeing life through a "We Matter" lens is that you will become highly aware of the fact that you have the power and capability to change lives of people you may never meet. One day, someone might be wearing your business outfit to interview for a job. One day a child will walk to school without holes in their shoes. This is the power of a culture of generosity. Congrats, you life-changer.

JOURNAL ENTRY

What is the most generous thing someone has ever done for you? How did it make you feel? Did it positively influence your level of generosity?

CONVERSATION STARTER

How do you think we can become a more generous society?

15

Be Bold
MAKE A STATEMENT

The meaning of life is to find your gift. The purpose of life is to give it away.

—Pablo Picasso

Pulling up to the arrivals area at any terminal at LAX is slightly dangerous and very annoying. The only way to describe it is "too many people and cars in too small of a space." This formula has never been my favorite, hence the reason I leave concerts before the final encore. That very last song is never worth the hour stuck in a parking lot, in my opinion.

What made this trip to LAX even more adventurous was that I had never met the person I was picking up. We had spoken on the phone a few times, but never met. Her name is Dr. Tererai Trent, and her story is one for the ages. From the pictures and videos I saw of her online, I knew I was picking up someone larger than life.

As I came back around on my ten-minute loop of LAX, I immediately spotted Tererai. There she stood in her traditional Zimbabwean headdress and dress. The colors were magnificent—different patterns going in different directions and creating a persona of power, style, and courage. I pulled my car right up in front of her and jumped out to meet her.

We only had a few hours to spend together before Tererai needed to return to the airport, so we went to a nearby hotel lobby, grabbed a table, and dove into conversation right away. It's amazing how within just moments I felt like I had known Tererai my entire life. It also felt like she had been alive for thousands of years, not because of her physical appearance, but because of her wisdom and the way she spoke. Her Zimbabwean accent was super thick as she rolled her R's and shifted the pronunciation of certain words. Her cadence was one of southern gospel preacher, almost as if every word carried with it animation and life. She was spellbinding.

Tererai grew up in the village of Zvipani in Zimbabwe. Unlike her brother, she was not allowed to get an education. Their culture believed that girls are for getting married and having babies, while boys are to become men and the breadwinners. Tererai shared with me that she would borrow her brother's books and try to learn at home on her own because she knew she would need to be educated to create a life for herself. She clearly had that desire for something more in her at a young age. When Tererai was just thirteen years old, her father sold her as a child bride in return for a cow, and by the age of eighteen, she already had three children.

Years later, Tererai met the leader of international affairs at Heifer International, a global nonprofit committed to ending poverty and hunger. Tererai was asked what her dreams were, and she shared that she wanted to move to America, get a bachelor's degree, a master's degree, and eventually a PhD. Her fifth and final dream was to then return to her village to build a school for girls and women. Tererai's mother told her that if she wrote her dreams down on a piece of paper and buried them in the ground, her dreams would grow to become true.

Her mother could not have been more correct. In her young thirties, Tererai moved to America and pursued and achieved all of her education goals. Her only remaining dream was to return and build the school, which became a reality when she appeared on *The Oprah Winfrey Show* and Oprah offered her $1.5 million to go back and build her school.

With my jaw on the ground in that airport hotel lobby, I struggled with what to say back to her. I knew there was something special about Tererai, but I wasn't exactly expecting that story. What a spirit. What a soul.

After sharing my story with her, Tererai sat for a moment and then said, "This is why we are supposed to meet.

You spend your days trying to help everyone know that they matter." The way she said "they matter" was so profound. She continued, "That I matter. That you matter. That we all matter. This is the same belief system that many of us in the African culture believe. It's called 'Ubuntu.'"

"Ubuntu means that 'I am through you.' That 'we are because of each other,'" she explained. "That my existence only matters through yours and vice versa. This is precisely your same message. It's so beautiful."

Our two hours together flew by in a minute. It was time to return Tererai to the airport, but we both knew this was just the beginning of something special.

Years prior to meeting Tererai, whom I now call "Vitamin T," I got the privilege of experiencing the African culture through the lives of two young boys. As part of my recovery from anxiety and depression, Denise also encouraged me to develop my faith. Armenia is said to be the first Christian nation. It is even believed that Noah's Ark is somewhere on a mountainside in Armenia to this very day. But I grew up in a family that believed in loving our neighbors and doing unto others as you would have others do unto you simply because it was the right way to live, not because of our religion.

As part of understanding what it meant to live a life that was not about me, Denise wanted me to look even bigger. I started going to church and reading the Bible and books by Wayne Dyer, the 14th Dali Lama, Desmond Tutu, Eckhart Tolle, Deepak Chopra, and so many other great spiritual and inspirational teachers. A big aspect of all of this exploration was that it started to allow me to surrender my need for control and to acknowledge that maybe, just maybe something bigger than me was in control here. It also grounded me and reconnected me to humanity. Anxiety and depression had shrunk my life so much that I felt completely alone and disconnected from everyone and everything. These learnings helped me feel like part of a larger fabric—the exact message behind Ubuntu and "We Matter."

One Sunday, at church, I saw a posting in the café that read CHAPERONES NEEDED. A children's choir from Uganda was coming to Los Angeles, and they needed hosts to take care of some of the children while in town. I signed up immediately and couldn't wait for the arrival of the new houseguests.

Two short months later, I drove to the church to meet my new friends, Joseph and Edwin. The boys were five and seven years, respectively, and were both orphans, having lost their families to civil war and the HIV epidemic. I also was assigned one of the adult leaders from the choir, whom they called "Uncle."

I spent five beautiful days with my guests, showing them the sights and sounds of Los Angeles. It was clearly something they were not accustomed to—the bright lights, massive portions of food, movie theaters, and all the hustle and bustle of people and automobiles. But they loved every second of it, which was amazing for me to experience.

Toward the end of their stay with me, I gave the two boys T-shirts that said YOU MATTER on them, and then asked if they knew what that meant. Of course we had some language barriers and cultural differences, so I needed to help the boys understand the context a little bit. Once they seemed to grasp it, I asked them, "Why do you matter?" Joseph said, "I matter because I love to dance and it makes people happy." Yes, he did. Joseph danced nonstop for the six days I was with him. He danced at dinner, while he brushed his teeth, while we watched TV. He was a dancing machine, and every single time I saw him dancing, I smiled and felt an overwhelming sense of joy. Edwin then shared, "I matter because one day I am going to change my country."

Again, this was a seven-year-old boy who lost both of his parents because of the unjust realities in his country, yet still had hope and a conviction to make things better. I was awestruck, yet challenged, for in that moment I reflected on how I would answer that question, and I didn't know the answer . . . yet.

Tererai, Joseph, and Edwin all had a profound impact on my life. Tererai taught me "Ubuntu." That yes, we do matter to one another. In fact, without each other we don't really matter at all. This is beyond profound and life- and world-changing. Life truly is a "we" thing, even when the "we" is on the opposite side of the world. I can still hear her beautiful voice saying, "I matter because of you. You matter because of me. We matter."

For Joseph and Edwin, I was supposed to be the one blessing them that week, but in the end, it was they who brought me so much joy and caused me to reflect on my own life. They helped me see that it's possible to have relatively nothing, by our materialistic standards, yet still be filled with joy, faith, and trust in a beautiful life. But most significantly of all, they also introduced me to Patty. For it was at the merchandise table after their concert that I bought an African necklace and gave it to this beautiful woman standing next to me with whom I have now spent the past ten years of my life.

"Hi, I'm Matt. I bought this for you."

"Hi, I'm Patty.

After Joseph and Edwin answered my question of "Why do you matter?" besides standing awestruck by their confident and concise answers, I was also scared to death. My honest thought was *holy crap, what if they turn around and ask me the same question? What would I say?* The truth is that I had no idea how I would have answered them and this got me thinking. I began to wonder if this would be a hard question for other people to answer as well, so, of course, I started asking people. No, I wouldn't just walk up to someone on the street and say, "Why do you matter?" But I did start asking friends, family members, and co-workers whether or not they ever pondered why they matter. Each time I asked the question, I received the same blank and curious expression, which told me everything I needed to know. . . . I wasn't the only person who would have struggled with this question.

What about you? What if I were to ask you why you matter? What would you say? How would it make you feel? My hope is that because of your journey with this book, you would be able to answer that question with ease. This is why I end every keynote I ever do the same way I am ending this book. Because answering the question "Why do you matter?" is the final action step of this book, but it is also the first step of living your new life. It is the opportunity for you to put all the pieces together and to truly own how much and why you matter. This is precisely why I wrote this book. For this moment. Because I have had the honor and privilege of watching thousands of people stand on a stage with me, in front of their peers, and share why they matter. It is the most transformational thing I have ever witnessed. So now it's your turn to finally own it. Yes, you matter. . . . You always have. And now it is time for you to proclaim it.

I want you to stand up, either by yourself or with others, and loudly and proudly complete the following statement:

My name is: _____

_____

I matter because: _____

_____

May this become your new personal mission statement. Your charge in life. Your north star. Feel it. Embrace it. Share it. And from this day forward, live every day knowing how much and why you matter . . . because you do.

Together we will change our own lives, the lives of others, and the world.

You matter.

TAKE ACTION

If I may be so bold to celebrate and share in your transformation, I would love to know how you completed your "I matter because . . ." statement. To help, I created the website: www.imatterbecause.com and the QR code below to make it super simple for you to share your statement with me and the world. All you need to do is scan the QR code with your phone and it will take you straight there. Not only will you be able to add your photo and statement, you will also get to relish in and experience a live mosaic of people from around the world who have shared their statements. Remember, we change the world from the inside out, and a world filled with people who know how much and why they matter is as good as it gets. I can't wait to meet you on the site.

JOURNAL PROMPT

Take a moment to write about the process you took as you created your final "I matter because . . ." statement. How did it feel? What emotions did you experience? Why? It's important to capture this moment on paper so you can revisit it whenever you need or want to.

CONVERSATION STARTER

Like I said, don't just start clobbering people with the "Why do you matter?" question. That is cruel and very overwhelming. But, as I did, just start to talk about the idea of mattering with people and get a sense of where they are. You might be the person that gets them started on this life-changing journey. Remember, your words matter. You matter.

A Final Framework

I am a visual learner, so I thought I would share this framework for you to see how the "I Matter," "You Matter," "We Matter" perspectives work together. For so many years, this is how I saw it:

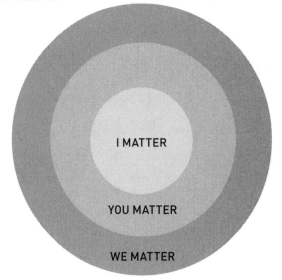

In a very rudimentary way, I saw the "I Matter" as the inner circle. That's our internal work. I saw the "You Matter" as the next ring around us. This is our ability to reach out and impact others in our close proximity. Then, I saw the "We Matter" as this larger ring around all of us that helps us connect to something even larger by understanding how powerful we are together and that we are all equal parts of this thing called humanity.

Then in spring of 2019, as the final piece to this book and nearly twenty years after my breakdown, the diagram shifted. I realized that the lines weren't so static. I started asking myself, "When are we in 'I Matterland' and not in 'You Matterland'?" Because serving someone else also serves me. Or, "Isn't time spent in 'You Matterland' also a good thing for 'We Matterland'?" For when we serve one, we are also serving the greater whole? And, as I sat at my desk, listening to Sigur Ros and seeing the flicker of the candle on the desk in the corner of my eye, a new diagram hit me:

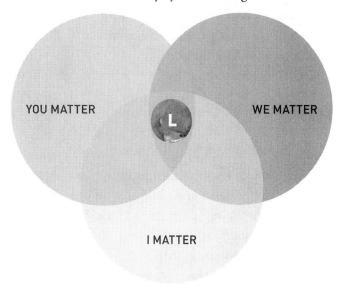

I realized that these three perspectives overlap one another and that we constantly weave our way among them throughout each day. We don't all come to them at the same place, and we don't stay in the same place. And alone they don't mean as much as they do together, which brings me to the small circle in the middle, where all of the perspectives overlap. The "L" represents "life." I believe that this is where we are meant to live—in constant connection with our "I," "you," and "we."

This is where we set boundaries, take care of ourselves, and honor our values.

This is where we embrace how powerful we are to impact others in our daily life.

This is where we do our part with and for one another to change the world.

This is how we all live a good life in a good world, filled with hope, purpose, promise, love, compassion, kindness, joy, meaning, and significance.

This is how we ultimately embrace how much and why we matter.

Thank you.

Thank you for giving of your precious time to take this journey with me. I don't take it lightly, and I want you to know how much it matters to me. As I said in the opening of this book, my ultimate goal was to help you understand how much and why you matter.

I hope that, in some small or really big way, I have

helped you embrace this. But I am also a realist. I know that this stuff takes work. We didn't find ourselves in our current place in life overnight, so it might take a second to shift away or transform from it. As you now know, it took me years. I don't share that to discourage you in any way, though, because those years, even the toughest ones, were the best years of my life. So much about living and thriving starts with being aware. Sadly, so many people aren't and they live their lives quasi-numb, quasi-clueless, and quasi-ill. I did it so very well. Maybe you did, too. But the good news is that we can all change . . . and you have already started that process.

Whether you know this consciously or not, you have always known that you matter, and I have proof of it— it's the simple fact that you are reading these words right this very second. If you didn't know you mattered, you wouldn't have been looking for more. You wouldn't believe more was possible. You wouldn't think you deserved more. But you did and you do, and that is one of the most encouraging and inspiring thoughts in the world to me.

You matter.

I would love to hear your "I matter because . . ." statement. Please use this QR code to share it with me and to join the mosaic of people from around the world who have done the same thing.

Acknowledgments

Every relationship, conversation, and experience throughout my life has impacted me . . . and therefore this book. This makes this part of the book beyond challenging, especially since I get limited space. All I can do is ask for grace.

Patty: This book would not have been written if it weren't for you. For years you encouraged me and wouldn't let me off the hook. I guess you were right; I did "have another book in me." Thank you for the brainstorming, proofreading, fresh-squeezed celery juice, and for sacrificing so much of our quality time together on the weekends and evenings to give me the space to write. This book is to and because of you. You have always been my biggest fan, best friend, and toughest critic. You fell in love with a dude who had a broken A/C in his car and asked you to join him at Subway for our first meal together. You are certainly a visionary. I am so grateful you chose and have stuck with me. I love doing life with you and our furry babies—Rooster, Rocky, and Rambo.

Mom and dad: I owe you everything. I will never know why I got so lucky to be born into this world with you as my parents. I am honestly the luckiest kid in the world. I know that if I was the first-born, I might have been an only child; but I also know that you have secretly enjoyed the color I bring to our family. Mom, I can hear you right now, "Matthew, only you!" filled with so much pride and excitement. Pops, thank you for always being our rock. I have leaned on your leadership and character and have stood on your shoulders, which allowed me to see and then become the man I am today. You are my best friends. You inspire me every day. I love you beyond words.

Michael: Even though you were the Golden Child, I still love you dearly, big brother. Thank you for your gentle kindness, laughter that makes your own eyes tear up, and jovial appreciation for the library of fart or poop books I have given you over the years. Also, thank you to my sister-in-law, Melissa, and my nephew and niece, Gavin and Kate. I love you so much. P.S. Michael, you broke the bed. Just admit it.

The Matoian family: Starting with grandma and grandpa, then Uncle Matty and Uncle John, and Chad and Brady and your families. I have always been so proud to be half Matoian. Thank you for your generosity; support and belief in me; and for always caring so deeply about people. Also to the extended Matoian family—the Shidan's, Minas', Shahbazian's, and Connor's. Thanksgiving and Christmas have always been so special because of you.

The Emerzian family. Starting with grandma and grandpa, then Auntie Barbara and Uncle Skip, and Geoff and Dana and your families. I'm sorry I didn't get any of your musical talents or thespian ways, but I have always appreciated them. Thank you for your constant love of and dedication to family. You are living examples that family matters most.

Momma Malcolm: Thank you for being the best mother-in-law ever. When you told me you were going to take me home and skin me alive when I snuck the cashier my credit card, I knew I loved you. Thank you to you and Victor for your daughter . . . my wife. And to the Malcolm and Co-thren families—I am honored to be part of your family.

Modesto, California: Thank you to all of my K-12 teachers. Each of you shaped me in some small way. To my childhood friends with whom I am still so close with today—Benak, Pfeifle, Bogger, Galli, Mooch, Damone, Blount, Schlub, Tooth, Jillbo, Priest, Lettuce, Barr, Oly, Chuckers, and so many others. To Sherwood Forest and Bristol Lane. And to all of our family friends . . . you have all supported and loved me, and our family, for so many years. I am forever grateful. Mr. Blount, I miss you and still hear you calling me "Big Dog" every day.

Los Angeles, California: Thank you to all of my friends and teammates at UCLA, including Coach Horn. To Andrew and Dave for your friendship and allowing me to be a part of your musical journey. To Virgil for your music and priceless memories. To everyone at the Regal Beagle for the countless laughs and endearing friendships. To Robert and all of the Kardashian family for giving a young music manager a shot. Robert, I think about you every single day and miss you greatly. To Bob for taking me under your wing after Robert passed away. To Kelly for writing the first Every Monday Matters book together and for your friendship. You were the only friend that knew about my dark days, and I cannot thank you enough for everything you did. To Denise, my "expensive friend" and life coach. Thank you for your time, patience, heart, faith, and for never giving up on me. You saved my life.

Every Monday Matters: Thank you to everyone who has played a role in the organization over the past ten years: Lamb, Muguet, Robin, Cindy, Ricardo, Kristin, Jocelyn, Lany, Jake, Nancy, Josh, James, Lauren, Meggan, Kami, Brent, Jennifer, Mia, Artyn, Lupe, Kathy, Graves, Rachel, Russell, Bill, Karen, Jill, Dundas, Steve, and Chris. To the thousands of educators and millions of students who are making their Mondays matter with our education program. We started in a small conference room in Modesto, California, and today we are in 49 states and 6 countries— Tom, Lori, Vicki, Nora, Christine, Oscar, Sheri, Mary Ann, Julie, Sherri, Danielle, Rick, Jim, Randy, Brent, Luis, Elena, Sandy, Mary Jo, Michelle, Michael, Mara, Tia, and so many more. To all of our corporate partners that are doing our corporate program and believe that their people matter most—Drew, Cammie, Ana, DPM, Jon, Margaret, Stephanie, Brent, Natalie, Mariam, Kathy, Jackie, Carol, Steve, Darin, Michael, and many other amazing leaders. To all of our donors, specifically to Kathy and the Jack in the Box Foundation; Alisha and the Living Legacy Foundation; Lenny and Allison and the Breeze Way Foundation; Brady and Chad and OK Produce; the David Weekley Family Foundation; the Matty Matoian Foundation; the Save Mart C.A.R.E.S. Foundation; the Scott and

Helen Graves Trust; E&J Gallo Winery; and the West and Gayner families. You have all gone above and beyond in supporting our education program and our youth. Thank you to my mentors and friends: Lenny, Tom, Shawn, Charles, David, Steve, Owen, and Rick. To Gabe and Rebekah and the Q and Axiom communities. To Dave and Josh and the Praxis Community. To the amazing ladies at Elle Communications. To Jack, Marc, and Mark and the TEDxSanDiego community for giving me a big stage to share my story.

Thank you to my tennis buddies: Goldie, Cortes, Anthony, Matt, Alex, Emi, Peter, Vernon, Eric, Rob, James, Ben, Dave, Mehran, Jeff, Mok, Lena, Jason, Tom, Tony, and so many others. You have blessed me with an unbelievable community. To the Turner family. I love you all so much. To Jay, Emily, and Eloise, for always asking how the book was coming since I became your invisible neighbor. To Jamma, for your friendship. To the Coyne family for your constant love and support throughout my entire life. To everyone I included in the stories throughout the book. You and your stories matter to me.

Thank you to Ken and John for writing the forward and preface to the book. Your words mean the world to me. You are amazing men, friends, and first-class world changers.

Thank you to my literary agent and friend, Christopher Ferebee, for believing in me and for working so hard with me on this book. To Jonathan and Angela for helping me sculpt and reveal the book I needed to write.

Thank you to Joel and Gwen at St. Martin's Press for welcoming me, and my family, into your publishing house. Joel, you taking the time to meet with me in person in order to truly understand my vision and me speaks volumes. I am truly honored and forever grateful. Your adoption papers are in the mail.

Finally to you, the person holding this book right now. Thank you for buying and for bringing life to my book. I truly hope it moves and transforms you. You matter.

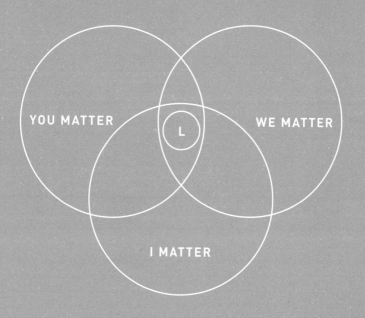

YOU MATTER

WE MATTER

L

I MATTER